POWER GENES

POWER GENES

Understanding Your **Power Persona**—
and How to Wield It at Work

MAGGIE CRADDOCK

Harvard Business Review Press

Boston, Massachusetts

Printed in the United States of America

10 9 8 7 6 5 4 3 2 1

No part of this publication may be reproduced, stored in or introduced into a retrieval system, or transmitted, in any form, or by any means (electronic, mechanical, photo-copying, recording, or otherwise), without the prior permission of the publisher. Requests for permission should be directed to permissions@hbsp.harvard.edu, or mailed to Permissions, Harvard Business School Publishing, 60 Harvard Way, Boston, Massachusetts 02163.

Library of Congress Cataloging-in-Publication Data

Craddock, Maggie.
    Power genes : understanding your power persona—and how to wield it at work /
Maggie Craddock.
        p. cm.
    ISBN 978-1-4221-6694-9 (hbk. : alk. paper)
    1. Control (Psychology) 2. Executive ability—Psychological aspects. 3. Management—Psychological aspects. 4. Industrial psychology. I. Title.
    HD38.2.C725 2011
    658.4'094—dc22

                                                                        2010045016

The paper used in this publication meets the requirements of the American National Standard for Permanence of Paper for Publications and Documents in Libraries and Archives Z39.48-1992.

This book is dedicated to the memory of Judy Tobias Davis.

She was a boundless source of grace and inspiration

to all who knew her

CONTENTS

1   Discovering Your Power Genes   1

2   Meet the Pleaser   25

3   Pleaser Power Plays   47

4   Meet the Charmer   63

5   Charmer Power Plays   83

6   Meet the Commander   101

7   Commander Power Plays   119

8   Meet the Inspirer   135

9   Inspirer Power Plays   157

10   Putting the Power Grid into Action   173

    Conclusion: Wielding Your Personal Power   193

    Notes   201
    Index   203
    Acknowledgments   211
    About the Author   215

CHAPTER ONE

Discovering Your Power Genes

Even the most talented and skilled professionals among us often don't grasp how to navigate the power dynamics that play out in many business situations.

As an executive coach, I've spent the last decade listening to the private thoughts and concerns of people on the cutting edge in business when it comes to the topic of power. Working with clients from around the world has taught me that, whether it's a CEO worried about being unseated by an aggressive board member or a business head trying to fend off the need to downsize hardworking employees, it simply isn't enough to try to help people think more strategically when power is on the line.

We've all seen it: the brilliant and highly trained business leader who bungles power. Not only does he or she fall from grace, but the fortunes of numerous colleagues whose livelihoods were tied to this leader hit the rocks as well. In hindsight, it seems unfathomable that someone so experienced and intelligent would make such a glaring misstep. It's as if this individual's ability to think logically were temporarily suspended. Many of us are glued to the headlines when this type of story breaks because we suspect that, embedded within the drama, there is a lesson—and an opportunity—here for all of us. It's not only titans at the top that have a lot to learn about the dynamics of power.

My experience has taught me that the way we wield and respond to power is not dictated by logic. Our instincts stem from how we were conditioned in the first system we experienced in life—our family system.

Whether you are trying to land a job or persuade an elusive client to pay an overdue bill, many of the reactions you have on the job stem from your automatic instincts around power. Our "power genes" kick in faster than the speed of thought. These automatic reactions, which in extreme situations can cause you to come across as either a dictator or a doormat, are rooted in behaviors you internalized when you were trying to get what you wanted as a child, long before you developed the capacity for individual discernment. A deeper understanding of power genes will enable you to deal more effectively with difficult people in the workplace and determine whether or not you can thrive in your current professional environment.

Managing power successfully requires a commitment. You can read about riding a motorcycle, and you can even watch movies and advertisements featuring other people riding, but you don't really know what it's all about until you get on the bike yourself. In a similar manner, learning to operate more powerfully on the job can't just be studied—it's something you learn by doing.

The power types I'll introduce in this book, the corresponding blind spots, and the reconditioning process I'll describe in chapter 10 will give you the insights and the action plan you need to become a more consistently powerful professional. Armed with this greater understanding of your own nature, you can learn to either leverage or bypass your power genes in order to be more effective and successful. With this enhanced awareness of what motivates your behavior, you have it within your reach to change and improve how you act in stressful situations. As you'll see, consciously managing your innate tendencies can be truly empowering.

A New Way of Looking at Power

My interest in family therapy began to blossom, of all places, on a Wall Street trading floor. During my previous career as a portfolio manager, I had experienced many moments when information was shared, and power was gained or lost, due to how people handled themselves in relation to the group energy created within their organizations. Noting when and why people did things that appeared to be at odds with their individual values due to pressure from their systems became a habit for me. At a Scudder, Stevens & Clark board meeting in New York, when the discussion turned to our search for an external hire to fill an important post, one of my colleagues whispered to me, "They can put Gandhi in that role, and if the system doesn't change, Gandhi will start acting crazy." As my fascination with the rise and fall of people in different systems began to eclipse my fascination with the rise and fall of assets in different markets, I eventually decided to leave financial services and pursue the training necessary to help people maximize their power on the job as well as their profit in the market.

My first book, *The Authentic Career,* gave readers a process for exploring the ways that their definitions of success, as well as the amount of money they needed to feel financially secure, were influenced by the values of their caregivers, siblings, lovers, and friends.[1] The popularity of this approach for clarifying the difference between your genuine desires and the goals others have suggested you "should" pursue gave me the opportunity to work with thousands of clients from around the world. Over the next several years, clients began to share with me how their family systems had not only influenced their career choices, but also shaped the ways they were conditioned to handle power struggles on the job.

Comparing my clients' early relationships with authority figures in their families with the relationships these same clients were having with authority figures in their current jobs unearthed some important trends. As I examined the patterns that recurred across different client groups, my findings became the basis for the Power Grid I introduce in this book.

We all have power genes, and they influence our behavior every day. Having won two Lipper Awards for excellence in portfolio management, I know that there is no substitute for good research when it comes to understanding an investment. Likewise, I've found that our personal success can be enhanced by uncovering how our personal relationship with power on the job mimics the power dynamics experienced in our family system.

The roots of family therapy stem from research in the field of biology. In 1945, Austrian-born biologist Ludwig von Bertalanffy presented his General Systems Theory. Bertalanffy's work was originally intended to explain the interrelatedness of organisms in ecosystems. However, after the world wars, anthropologists such as Margaret Mead and Gregory Bateson began applying these principles to social systems and postulating that interactive patterns among people should become a central focus for the study of human development. Prior to this, the dominant thinking in this sphere was led by therapists such as Sigmund Freud and Carl Rogers, who focused on working with people individually and isolating them from destructive family influences.

By the 1960s, systems theory had become so widely accepted in the social sciences that it was evolving into a new branch of psychotherapy, and family systems theory was born. Virginia Satir expanded on the concept of how individuals behave and communicate in groups by describing several roles she believed were characteristic in most family systems, including the hero, the scapegoat, and the lost child. By the 1970s, family systems theory had become so widely accepted that psychoanalyst Nathan Ackerman was able to found an institute dedicated to this approach. I had the pleasure of studying at the Ackerman Institute in the 1990s.

According to the classical family systems theory as defined by pioneers in this field such as Salvador Minuchin, the parents define the core subsystem of authority in any family.[2] As children are born, the family expands and sibling subsystems evolve. The flow of power throughout the family system is modeled by the way that the parents share power with one another. When parents are able to resolve conflicts fairly within their own subsystem, and then model the spirit of mutual respect and healthy compromise for their children, the archetypal family system where power is dealt with in a healthy manner is established. However, whenever children's needs are either underemphasized or overemphasized, and particularly in situations where children get inadvertently dragged into power struggles between their parents, less functional patterns for giving and taking power may be internalized.

What experience has taught me is that these less functional patterns for getting what we want and need don't just play themselves out on the schoolyard; they live on inside all of us and eventually play themselves out on the job. When a manager's negative or ineffective behavior is triggered by a high-stress relationship or situation on the job, the internal response—whether driven by trust or fear—is often rooted in the conditioned responses learned in the family system. When we view our professional style conflicts through the lens of the family framework, we develop empathy and insight into our own and others' behavior.

As we watch the rise and fall of public figures such as Bernie Madoff and Eliot Spitzer, we realize that no amount of influence over others can make up for a lack of insight into our own psyches. How could these men have gained so much power over others but lost so much power over themselves? Did their respective addictions to material gain and high-risk sexual encounters stem from the fact that they didn't feel as powerful on the inside as they tried to look on the outside? To what extent did their early experiences in their family systems contribute to their ability to rationalize their high-risk behavior? Did they think they were above the law, or were they replaying behavior they had seen modeled in their family systems? While these are admittedly sensational examples, they emphasize a vital point about power: it is through achieving a balance between the behavior we employ to control people and situations outside us and the emotional forces driving us from within that authentic power is established and maintained.

Many of us lose our sense of balance around power in more subtle ways. Perhaps we become overly focused on gaining another's approval or fall into a pattern of micromanagement under stress. Whatever your pattern is, understanding how the early conditioning you experienced in your family system has shaped your response to power can prepare you to weather stressful situations without risking your reputation, your marriage, and, ultimately, your financial security.

A Few Words About Words

For the purposes of this book, I'm defining *power* as the ability to chart your own professional course rather than having this direction dictated to you by forces beyond your control. This definition has implications for your relationships with others, your contract with the organizations you join, and even how you feel about yourself.

As far as your relationship with yourself is concerned, this use of power denotes the strength to distinguish your true values and intentions from the objectives endorsed by the various influencers that are around you. In terms of your relationships with others, power used in this context indicates the ability to deal with conflict in a way that fortifies your personal integrity rather than diminishing it. Finally, this definition of power denotes the ability to actively support organizations and situations that reinforce your core values and, when necessary, to make a break with those that don't.

As we shall see, when it comes to power, the most important conflicts we have in business are often the conflicts we have within ourselves. By coming to understand the roots of our style differences, what I call our power genes, each of us can learn to operate more powerfully on the job.

Since the term *power genes* builds from this definition of power, it also has tripartite implications. This book employs the term *power genes* to refer to the conditioned responses, both emotional and behavioral, that an individual has internalized based on ongoing exposure to the operating style of the authority figures in his or her family.

Genes, which we are born with, can be recessive or dominant, depending on a complex maze of factors. Since the word *genes* semantically plays to the biological nature we are born with, this word is not meant to be interpreted in isolation or taken literally. Our use of the term *power genes* relates to how each of us was *nurtured*. This book refers explicitly to the ways that our most primal responses concerning power were habitually reinforced by the caregivers who raised us. Like genes, these conditioned responses are often passed on unconsciously from one family generation to the next. As you will see, understanding the notion and dynamics of power genes can serve as an effective metaphor for how you have been emotionally and behaviorally conditioned—keeping in mind the obvious limitations of the terminology. The ways that your power genes influence your relationships and dictate how well you "fit" in a particular organization are the main topics of this book.

The Power Grid

To understand power at a basic level, it's important to understand the building blocks that we all draw from. These are our internal emotional drives and the external behavior we exhibit in the world around us. Both have their genesis in the ways we were conditioned to get what we wanted in our family systems.

FIGURE 1-1

The Power Grid

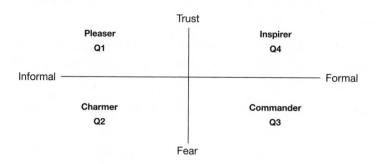

I've found that an individual's relationship with power predominantly falls into one of four categories. These categories can be sorted according to the simple two-by-two matrix in figure 1–1.

Understanding the Y-Axis

The y-axis measures our emotional reflexes, which can range from seeking trust at one end of the spectrum to reacting out of fear at the other. These reflexes, which kick in faster than the speed of thought, are emotionally hardwired into us based on our early experiences with the authority figures who raised us.

People who operate near the trust end of the spectrum a high percentage of the time tend to comply when they feel included and appreciated. A trust-based power style is defined by a tendency to seek other's opinions and strive for consensus—even if reaching consensus is time consuming. Energy and attention flow openly between people when trust-based power is invoked. People who operate at this far extreme of the y-axis often struggle with logic as they have a tendency to personalize professional issues. Unless they are able to separate their need for validation from their professional responsibilities, they are often unable to perform at their peak.

In contrast, people who operate near the fear end of the y-axis invoke a power style characterized by a tendency to avoid full disclosure, to foster a sense of urgency, and to establish an imbalance of power. Energy and attention flow as commanded when fear-based power is invoked. People who operate at the fear-based extreme of the y-axis often struggle with nuance. Unless they are given clear-cut directions and formal orders, plus consequences for noncompliance, they often aren't motivated to perform.

To see how the y-axis affects how we both give and take power, consider the classic example of the commanding colleague who likes to believe he deals with power in an inspirational manner. When he gets feedback, he is baffled by how many of his reports claim they are intimidated by him and are reluctant to be candid with him about business challenges in a timely manner. If he is operating near the fear-based extreme of the y-axis, he will have a naturally higher tolerance for confrontation and aggression than others whose family systems might map them closer to the trust end of the y-axis. Thus, in terms of how this individual responds to power, it will take a strong sense of urgency to get his attention. In terms of how he wields power, he may honestly believe that he is being diplomatic, while many people who work with him may experience his behavior as unpleasantly direct.

Understanding the X-Axis

The x-axis of the Power Grid characterizes the behavioral style that an individual gravitates toward to influence others. People who operate near the informal end of the x-axis have a preference for one-on-one interactions with others to get what they want. Individuals who gravitate toward the informal end of the x-axis often got their needs met early in life by making an individual appeal to one of the authority figures in their family system. On the job, these individuals tend to echo what worked for them early in life by establishing a preference for individual meetings and one-on-one conversations when dealing with anything from a strategic brainstorming session to a marketing pitch.

In contrast, people who operate near the formal end of the x-axis have a natural tendency to work with systems to further their ambitions. People who gravitate toward the formal end of the x-axis often developed a flair for tapping into the group energy of their family system to get their needs met. As I explained in my first book, *The Authentic Career*, group energy can be thought of as the way that the dominant thought patterns and associated reactions established by the most influential members of any system work together to create an emotional tone that establishes its own distinct energy. In the family system, we can work with group energy by getting the support of our siblings or managing the airwaves between our parents. On the job, whether they are invoking their credentials or their seniority or even drawing on the natural charisma they exude in front of an audience or group, individuals who operate at the formal end of the x-axis have a tendency to think in terms of how the group is going to react as they seek to realize their ambitions.

One point worth noting is that if you have seniority within an organization, by virtue of your job description you will be required to deal with group energy more than someone who doesn't have the responsibility of numerous reports. So it may seem as if people who are in positions of seniority in an organization have more "formal" power because they are required to tap into the group to execute their job requirements. This point illustrates why it can be important to beware of snap judgments in terms of how you categorize your own power style or that of someone you work with. For example, some people in senior management roles are uncomfortable dealing with groups and, as a result, struggle with business situations where a more formal power style is required. Such senior executives may be terrific rainmakers if they are able to close deals in one-on-one settings with important clients. However, if these same senior executives struggle with a tendency to isolate and don't stay plugged in to the day in and day out nuances of what's going on with the group energy of people who report to them, they can find management responsibilities challenging.

The Power Quadrants

The Power Grid, which is the result of combining the x- and y-axes described above, provides a framework to understand the interplay of your internal emotional reflexes and your external behavioral preferences. Mapping yourself on the Power Grid not only enhances your awareness of how your early conditioning may be affecting your current behavior on the job, it also clarifies why people operating from other quadrants on the grid might respond favorably to your power style—or not. Clarifying the quadrant or quadrants you operate from most frequently can give you the insight you need to deal with difficult people and situations more powerfully and move ahead on the job.

The Pleaser

As we examine the power style of the Pleaser, we will consider individuals who have honed their ability to make others feel good about themselves but struggle with an ongoing hunger for validation and approval. Pleasers rarely make the headlines because they are so busy supporting those around them—often at their own expense. However, as we consider the background of Cynthia Cooper, a whistle-blower at WorldCom, we will watch what happens as a Pleaser's innate drive to take care of the details others may overlook causes her to unearth something that ultimately forces her to break ranks and risk the disapproval of the authority figures in her corporate system.

Pleasers operate near the trust-based end of the y-axis because they are constantly looking to others to validate them.

Behaviorally, Pleasers prefer one-on-one interactions. After all, when you deal with groups, you might have to risk the disapproval of someone, and Pleasers want everyone to like them. The preference for individual interactions puts Pleasers at the informal end of the x-axis. As we examine the power style of the Pleaser more thoroughly in chapters 2 and 3, we will see how the sense of scarcity that Pleasers grow up with fosters the emotional and behavioral triggers that compel them to operate from this quadrant under pressure.

The Charmer

The power style of the Charmer exemplifies people who project an image that is able to both seduce and intimidate others. Charmers hide behind their images because early childhood experiences have made it difficult for them to trust others. As we reflect on the rise, fall, and rebound of Darryl Strawberry, we will see how some Charmers will go to such extreme lengths to run from their inner demons that even they aren't aware of what's driving them.

Charmers exude an emotional intensity that keeps everyone around them slightly anxious. Due to the emotional tone they convey, Charmers operate near the fear-based end of the y-axis.

Behaviorally, Charmers find it easier to seduce and/or manipulate others by approaching people individually. If they were dealing with a group, their talent for selectively conveying information or creating private alliances might unravel. Thus, Charmers operate at the informal end of the x-axis. As we take a closer look at the Charmer's power style in chapters 4 and 5, we will explore the ways that Charmers have become falsely empowered in their family systems. The emotional and behavioral triggers that condition a Charmer are often unconsciously fostered by a caregiver who needed the young Charmer to "parent" them.

The Commander

The Commander exemplifies the power style that is most commonly associated with the military, leaders of industry, and heads of state. While the Commander's ability to take charge decisively often garners widespread admiration, they are often gripped by the fear of losing control. One of America's most well-known CEOs, Jack Welch, provides a rich example of the possibilities and challenges inherent in this traditional leadership style.

Commanders, who feel anxious about anything that might prevent them from being in charge at all times, operate near the fear-based end of the y-axis.

Behaviorally, Commanders are constantly evaluating where they fall within the hierarchy of their system. Their innate skill for dealing with groups, and their penchant for constantly assessing their own standing within the group, causes them to operate at the formal end of the x-axis. As we explore the power style of the Commander in chapters 6 and 7, we will see how the emotional and behavioral triggers that condition Commanders get forged in hierarchical family systems, where power is always related to your place in the pecking order.

The Inspirer

The Inspirer exemplifies star power in action. The Inspirer is able to tap into the deep longing we all have to find a sense of meaning through supporting something greater than ourselves. That said, the Inspirer can get derailed when his or her vision for the future eclipses a realistic appreciation of the tactical dangers in the present. As we consider the metamorphosis of Jimmy Carter from president of the United States to his current role as a thought leader and humanitarian, we can see how the same idealism that undermined his political career served to fortify his commitment to building a sustainable platform for serving the American people.

Inspirers, examined in chapters 8 and 9, are emotionally drawn to support a cause that they consider greater than themselves. Their faith in this cause, and their support of others who share their sense of commitment, causes them to operate near the trust-based end of the y-axis.

Behaviorally, Inspirers operate with a sense of ease with people from all walks of life. The natural charisma they exude in any group puts them at the formal end of the x-axis. As we examine the family background of the Inspirer, we will see how the emotional and behavioral triggers that condition someone to operate from this quadrant are fostered in a system where spontaneity is valued over structure and creativity is considered more important than conformity.

Pros and Cons of the Quadrant Approach

The way each quadrant has been titled is intended as a teaching device to help personify the way that the emotional and behavioral forces come together to exemplify a particular power style. Like any teaching device, naming these quadrants has pros and cons.

The downside of personifying the quadrants is that some readers may misunderstand this attempt to breathe life into these four power styles and make the snap judgment that we are trying to categorize people based on emotional and behavioral triggers. Beware of the pitfall of categorizing too starkly your own power style or that of someone you are dealing with. The purpose of this framework is to begin an important dialogue concerning the building blocks of power we all have at our disposal. A deeper insight into the many ways power can be wielded can free us to operate with more agility and draw from a wider range of strategic responses at important turning points in our lives and careers.

Many clients have told us that working with the Power Grid has helped them incorporate other models and tools, such as Myers-Briggs, more comprehensively. For example, while Myers-Briggs gives people a valuable snapshot of their most predominant operating style, it provides little insight into how an individual's personal history will allow them to optimize this style. By using the Power Grid in conjunction with tools such as Myers-Briggs, you'll gain a deeper insight into how your personal history has shaped many of your habitual responses.

Through developing a deeper understanding of the roots of your habitual reactions, you'll be able to incorporate the results of other well-known standardized testing tools into an action plan for developing more agile and effective responses on the job.

As you develop a fuller sense of how the quadrants on the Power Grid are defined, bear in mind that the quadrant that you or one of your colleagues operates from most of the time is not a reflection of morals. There are no "good" or "bad" quadrants. Each has its virtues and its blind spots, and each style on the grid has important lessons to help us all become more conscious of how power plays can work themselves out between different types of people in the workplace. As you study these contrasting power styles, you will gradually become more facile working with a framework that doesn't stop at how you think about critical situations; the Power Grid helps you dig deeper to explore the automatic reactions that kick in on the job when you are too anxious, or possibly too exhausted, to think at all.

As a framework, the Power Grid is intended to help us all begin an important conversation with ourselves. It is not the first or the last word on the subject. As important as this framework has been for my clients, a myriad of additional factors—ranging from an individual's level of personal wealth to their physical beauty or even their biochemical disposition—can add dimensions to this framework. What's more, as you will see throughout this book, the Power Grid itself was created by taking some of the core concepts developed by talented family systems practitioners and applying them in a coaching capacity to the most common challenges people encounter in professional systems.

As we reflect on the most common career challenges we tend to face, it's important to note that the quadrant in which you operate depends on the situation you are facing. Many of us can operate from more than one quadrant in the course of a given day. For example, a CEO who operates from the Commander quadrant and rules with an iron fist with his executive committee may find himself operating from the

Pleaser quadrant and walking on eggshells with an important board member.

Through an honest self-evaluation, described in chapter 10, of how the patterns that operated in your family system influence where you may fall on this grid, you will learn to master the challenges presented by your current blind spots around power—and also clarify how others give and take power in your presence.

Common Concerns

Before exploring the individual power styles in more detail throughout this book, I'll mention the three common concerns I've encountered when teaching people how to use this framework.

How Much Time Will This Take?

Many clients are concerned that this type of personal evaluation will take too much time. Some have confessed that they associate self-examination with spending countless hours in therapy and that the time commitment is not a realistic option for them.

The good news is that the Power Grid framework can be put into practice quickly and can have a positive impact on the countless hours you already devote to relational challenges on the job. What's more, many people report that this process works fast because it helps them clarify what, deep down, they have already suspected to be true about themselves. Many of us spend a tremendous amount of energy filtering out information that would upset the balance of power as it was initially established in our family systems. Working with the Power Grid helps you take your inner operating system off automatic pilot so you can reconnect with your genuine instincts and trust them to guide you. Clients who are initially the most guarded are frequently the same ones who report being amazed at how quickly this framework has helped them strengthen their power base on the job.

Will This Make Me Uncomfortable?

Some clients tell me they are reluctant to try this because looking within is just too painful. Many of them have spent years arming themselves with excuses and social distractions to avoid the pain of dealing with the feelings associated with their past. They believe that they will be more comfortable if they keep their personal feelings and their professional behavior in separate camps.

One reason I created this framework is that, in my experience, it's virtually impossible to separate who you are as a person from how you operate as a professional. In addition, it's far less painful to confront head-on the way that our past conditioning may be influencing our professional effectiveness than to stay trapped in cycles of self-defeating behavior.

If This Works, Why Aren't We Already Doing It?

Finally, many clients have asked me why this technique, if it's so effective, isn't being put into practice in a more widespread way in the workplace.

The number one reason people are reluctant to get to the root of what is sabotaging their relationship with power is that they are afraid they can't change. Who wants to nail the root causes of why they are being underpaid or operating ineffectively as a manager if they feel they can't fix the problem once they have identified it?

The main reason I've taken the insights from our corporate workshops and put them into a book is that, having helped numerous clients navigate this framework, I've seen how consistently people operate far more powerfully by understanding these principles. It's frequently the clients who protest, "That's just the way I am, I can't change!" who are the most relieved to discover that we can all change the way we've been conditioned to respond to power, once we learn the root causes of our automatic responses.

How Power Genes Play Out on the Job

The case study of Larry illustrates how power genes can influence career momentum.

The head of corporate communications for an investment firm, Larry had built his power base on the strong relationships he had developed with business journalists—they kept his firm's name out of the headlines when the news was bad, and made sure his organization was mentioned when upbeat stories were featured. As a reward for his success, the CEO of the firm was considering promoting Larry to partner. Since no one from corporate communications had been elevated to this level of seniority in the past, Larry would need to be informally vetted by the other partners at the firm to make sure that he "fit in" at the senior executive level.

Larry was elated. He was also terrified. This potential promotion thrust Larry into the spotlight on the job in a way that made him feel extremely self-conscious.

While Larry had extensive experience coaching the existing senior partners to talk to reporters, he felt as tongue-tied as a new kid on the first day of school when it came to the endless small talk and informal bonding necessary to establish himself as an insider among the senior partners at his firm. What was his task? Where were the formal instructions to show him what he needed to do? When the CEO drew him into an informal chat with some of the other senior partners at an off-site breakfast meeting, Larry could feel his power draining away. To prove he was worthy of the attention of the leaders surrounding him, he started babbling anxiously about his latest media campaign.

Power is often established in the informal moments between people, where there is no official script to follow. After a few awkward conversations with the other partners, where the CEO was forced to throw Larry a conversational life preserver to keep him from drowning, Larry realized he needed to do something fast. If he didn't, he risked being passed over because he couldn't manage to set the tone expected of senior leaders in the firm.

Initially, Larry was skeptical when I suggested we look at how his pattern of losing power in informal networking situations might be connected to experiences from his family system. He half jokingly tried to brush me off by saying, "Look, I've been in therapy. We don't have time for this. I have a promotion on the line, and the clock is ticking." That said, once Larry admitted that he couldn't seem to "think" his way out of this problem, he began to accept that the reason he was losing power might not be rooted in logic—it might be rooted in conditioning.

How Family History Codes Our Power Genes

Larry's father, Seth, was a mechanic who supported his family by running his own car repair business. His mother, Bethany, was trained as an accountant and kept the books for his father's business. Larry's parents worked hard to make ends meet and to pull together to deal with life's challenges.

The biggest challenge the family faced during Larry's childhood was his older brother, Craig, who started out as a top student and athlete and then fell from grace when he got involved with drugs and alcohol. Over time, the family system began to revolve around whether Craig was in or out of jail and how they were going to find the funds to get Craig into the next rehab.

The pressure Larry felt to make sure his family "looked good" on the outside as the strain of Craig's mounting problems grew on the inside transformed Larry into a skilled "spin doctor" at an early age. His family's central challenge became the genesis of some of Larry's most powerful skills. To keep the tension manageable when Craig was in crisis, Larry learned how to field calls from concerned school officials, medical professionals, and even curious relatives when his parents were too overwhelmed with their own grief to communicate with the outside world.

When it came to his role in the family system, Larry was transformed into a caretaker as well as a communicator. He paid a high price learning how to play this role. No matter how perfect his grades were or how hard he worked to support his parents, Larry's accomplishments always seemed to be eclipsed by Craig's latest setback. Over time, Larry developed a deep longing to have his own voice acknowledged and heard. In fact, he wanted to be heard so badly that he ended up going into communications for a living.

As with any appetite that grows out of control, Larry found that his longing for attention from his parents was so enduring that it was eventually transferred onto the authority figures he encountered in the systems he became part of later in life. Thus, in spite of his intelligence and experience, Larry inadvertently panicked every time he seemed to be losing the approval of the partners he longed to impress. When the fear of losing the positive attention he craved washed over him, a vicious cycle kicked in where Larry's mind went blank, he became progressively more anxious, and his personal power took a nosedive.

Another dimension of the challenge was that Larry's experience with the authority figures in his family system had conditioned him to seek validation but never find it. The realization that this promotion might give him the recognition he had always craved was unsettling because it was outside the parameters that his parents had inadvertently conditioned him to settle for. Unable to make logical sense of why he was losing power when he needed it the most, Larry was baffled by his own self-destructive behavior.

Working with the Power Grid

By becoming aware of the ways he had been conditioned to react in his family system, Larry was able to grasp why he became overly anxious when he felt that the authority figures surrounding him were withholding their attention. Once he came to terms with the realization that validation from his parents had been a lifelong craving for him, it was easier for him to accept why he often became so flooded with emotion at the prospect of losing favor with the authority figures around him that his brain seemed to flatline.

Like all of us, once Larry was able to connect his pattern of losing power in business situations with the central challenges he had grappled with in his family, he started to understand his power genes clearly enough to begin the process of consciously reconditioning himself. For Larry, this reconditioning involved acknowledging the feelings that cropped up inside him when he started babbling anxiously, stopping to take a deep breath and finding a humorous way to put himself and those around him at ease. As we shall see, for people struggling with other types of blind spots, this reconditioning may involve skills ranging from strengthening your confidence in your own instincts under pressure to learning to moderate outbursts of frustration.

The good news is that Larry got his promotion. During the cocktail reception, the CEO told Larry that his ability to operate more powerfully in informal moments had been a crucial factor in his advancement. As Larry learned, developing a deeper awareness of ways he had been coded to inadvertently give his power away and what he needed to do to reclaim it wasn't just about improving his social skills. Once he made partner, Larry quickly learned that he was going to have to protect his budget and his turf as his new peers tried everything from charm to confrontation to get what they wanted from him. Through grasping the ways that his own relationship with power was rooted in his early experiences with the authority figures in his family, Larry found that he was prepared to react more consciously to the power plays others might adopt to exert their influence on the job.

As Larry's story demonstrates, it's the emotional and behavioral triggers established in our family systems that often determine whether we lash out in anger or seek a deeper level of understanding when our power is being threatened in the systems where we seek professional advancement.

Getting Started

The chapters that follow describe the power quadrants in more detail, including the strengths and weaknesses associated with each. I will go on to explore the ways your patterns around giving and receiving power influence your behavior in three key relational dynamics where power is exchanged in the workplace: managing up, managing down, and managing across. Finally, in chapter 10, I'll offer a practical framework for reconditioning the power genes that control your actions and reactions.

As you'll see, each chapter contains stories of individuals who fall within each quadrant and the challenges they face. While some identifying details have been altered to protect confidentiality, these are all true stories. As you reflect on the case studies, try to remain mindful of the emotional reactions these stories may trigger in you as well as the ways these feelings serve to deepen or dilute the quality of the inner dialogue you have with yourself concerning power.

Throughout the book I will describe how you can use this awareness to change your behavior in order to:

- Deal with difficult people and situations in your current job more effectively.

- Identify work environments that reward individuals who exhibit your interpersonal instincts.

- Make the behavioral changes necessary to assess whether you can achieve your professional ambitions in your current work environment, or whether it's time for a transition.

- Communicate the value of the contributions you are making within your organization more clearly and persuasively.

As you read on, remember to be patient with yourself. Most of your life has been focused on reinforcing the conditioning you experienced in your family system. With greater focus, you'll develop insight into when you are thinking logically and when you are operating from your blind spots. The real payoff happens as you gradually develop the agility you need to apply your newfound insights with dignity and authority.

CHAPTER TWO

Meet the Pleaser

As a highly successful head of client service once told me, "When you can make others feel great about themselves in your presence, that's power!" Whether they are creating a top-notch research report or forging a strong business alliance, highly sensitive Pleasers innately understand that their success doesn't rest on how they come across—it rests on making others feel good about themselves when they interact with them.

Pleasers can be masterful at wielding power through others. Their power genes allow them to rise to leadership positions most easily in nonhierarchical cultures due to their ability to manage a large workload without sacrificing their empathy for others in the process. What's more, their attention to detail makes Pleasers integral to many of our most complex and influential organizations. The ongoing press concerning business corruption has raised awareness concerning Pleasers in regulatory roles who have played a heroic role reviving the moral compass of big business. Cynthia Cooper, the loyal and diligent whistle-blower during the WorldCom scandal, is one of the people frequently cited in our workshops as exemplifying the power style of a Pleaser. Other people who seem to exemplify the Pleaser's ability to lead by drawing out the humanity in others include humanitarian Thich Nhat Hanh, author Elie Wiesel, and Mother Teresa.

Nobel Prize–winning author Elie Wiesel's inner life, like that of many Pleasers, was shaped by his longing for the attention of an elusive caregiver—in Wiesel's case, this was his father. In the opening to his memoirs, *All Rivers Run to the Sea,* Wiesel uses his gift of language to express the type of yearning that drives the accomplishments of many gifted Pleasers: "I never really knew my father. It hurts to admit that, but it would hurt even more if I deluded myself. The truth is I knew little of the man I loved most in the world, the man whose merest glance could stir me . . . What was he thinking as he stared in silence at some far-off, invisible point in space? Why did he conceal his cares and disappointments from me? Because I was too young, or because he thought me incapable (or worse) of comprehending them?"[1]

As with many Pleasers, the sense of emotional scarcity created by an elusive caregiver left Wiesel with more questions than answers when it came to his sense of identity early in life. Due to his literary brilliance, Wiesel was able to transform this longing into a plethora of publications on the human condition that speak to longing for connection in us all.

While it is unsurprising that Pleasers are often drawn to the helping professions, such as counseling and philanthropy, many of them actually work in some of our most competitive private sector organizations. As many as 55 percent of the clients we have worked with in *Fortune* 500 companies have told us in interviews that they consider themselves Pleasers. Being a Pleaser doesn't necessarily dictate the career you choose; but it can define how you progress and perform in that career.

Strengths of the Pleaser

As you'll see, there's a lot to like about the Pleaser. It is a good thing so many of us fall into this power quadrant—their actions in support of others are often the critical building blocks that bolster an organization.

Highly Intuitive

One of the strongest characteristics we associate with Pleasers is their ability to intuit what will put others at ease. This skill is the foundation of the Pleaser's ability to wield power through others and often lands them in the position of being the go-to person for a top client or even a CEO. The Pleaser's intuitive talent often stems from the way he or she learned to read the needs of caregivers who were too busy or preoccupied to state what they needed directly.

Their capacity for empathy gives Pleasers an edge when it comes to dealing with the human element in business. The uncanny thing about Pleasers is that they may know what you need before you do. Add to this the fact that many Pleasers have been conditioned to pitch in diligently to meet others' needs without waiting for an invitation, and you've got someone who goes beyond giving you what you want—a Pleaser often anticipates your requirements. For example, a savvy Pleaser will know the perfect moment to prep the busy CEO dashing down the hall on how to handle a tense investor relations call. It's not uncommon to see Pleasers working the room at a fund-raiser and instinctually knowing how to handle the donors who couldn't be seated at the head table. While Inspirers are also facile networkers, their focus tends to be on the group's mission. The Pleaser, in contrast, is more likely to zero in on what each individual needs to feel special—one person at a time.

Cynthia Cooper's autobiography, *Extraordinary Circumstances*, is a true story that often reads like a suspense thriller.[2] As the drama reaches its climax, Cooper's intuition becomes one of her key survival skills as she is forced to navigate the treacherous waters of whom to trust and what to do while getting misinformation and even threats from those around her. At one point, when Cooper begins operating on instinct in terms of when to engage and when to literally hide from people pursuing her, this true story begins to resonate with the suspense of a spy novel. In the end, it was Cooper's ability to trust her gut that enabled her to survive and expose the corruption surrounding her. Later, as the public began to grasp the insight and dedication it took for this sensitive employee to stand up to a big corporation, *Time* magazine made the editorial decision to feature Cooper, along with whistle-blowers Sherron Watkins from Enron and Coleen Rowley from the FBI, on its cover for Persons of the Year in 2002.

Good Listeners

The ability to listen in such a way that others actually feel heard is one of the most nurturing things one human being can do for another in a professional setting. Another signature quality of Pleasers is their ability to focus their entire being on taking in what another person is trying to communicate. This skill often makes Pleasers successful at managing a broad range of complex personalities.

A gifted Pleaser makes listening an art form. While Inspirers can be great listeners as well, the Inspirer is usually focused on the big picture, while the Pleaser tends to be nurturing a more personal connection with others. Pleasers don't just listen with their ears, they listen from the gut. They register much more than the words shared with them. A seasoned Pleaser will be conscious of your vocal tone, the pace of your speech, whether or not you repeat key phrases, your body language, and, most important, what you don't say, so that they get past your words to the deeper issue of what you actually *mean*. Thus, having a Pleaser on your task force or negotiation team can be the equivalent of having a secret weapon on your side.

Hardworking

It's the Pleasers on the team who will burn the midnight oil for the firm while other types on the grid have checked out to head for the gym. As long as they feel acknowledged, Pleasers will often be the first people at the office in the morning and the last to go home at night. Most

Pleasers have a highly developed sense of responsibility that compels them to make sure the job gets done. This makes them great coworkers and fabulous subordinates.

As we'll explore in more detail later, the Pleaser's tireless work ethic was often fostered in a family system where they were accustomed to scarcity and conditioned to give more than they got. In her autobiography, Cynthia Cooper gives an insider's perspective of the world of internal audit, where it's not uncommon for professionals to face big demands and get little recognition. As we reflect on the power style of the Pleaser, it's helpful to consider how Cooper's early experiences in her family system contributed to her ability to hang on in a position where she was eventually able to uncover one of the largest accounting frauds in corporate history.

Cooper recalls her mother, who went to secretarial school, telling her, "I've always had to work for peanuts."[3] Cooper goes on to explain how important it was to her not to disappoint her parents, when she writes, "I know all too well the sacrifices they are making for me, living paycheck to paycheck, sometimes rushing around town to pay the utility bills so they won't be cut off."

Cooper's later career is replete with situations where in spite of being given few resources and little appreciation, she kept her nose to the grindstone. Like many Pleasers, Cooper was able to persevere in a job that other power types might have exited because her family system had conditioned her to endure. Frankly, an Inspirer probably would have walked off the field long before a Pleaser like Cooper raised her nose from the grindstone to question what was going on around her. When she was snubbed or treated unfairly by one of her superiors, Cooper's initial reaction was to just keep trying harder.

Superb Diplomats

The Pleaser's intuitive talents, listening skills, and capacity for hard work come together to make them natural diplomats. Seeing a Pleaser mediate a conflict can feel like watching someone pull out a decoder ring to solve a puzzle. This is because the Pleaser is able to tap into the emotional needs of both parties and find a way to soothe frayed feelings as well as balance competing interests at a more logical level. Whether they are mediating a turf war or talking an irate client off a ledge, the Pleaser is often able to diffuse tension by making everyone on the battlefield feel appreciated and acknowledged. One hedge fund CEO I worked with, who is a self-identified Pleaser, consistently drew on his diplomatic skills to hold his firm together when a war broke out between the seed investors and the managing partners of his growing investment firm. When a peace accord was finally achieved, employees throughout the organization acknowledged that without having a tireless and sensitive negotiator at the helm, their firm would probably have blown up. It's worth noting that Charmers can also be topflight negotiators, but Charmers often try to shape the presentation of the facts to suit their own ends. Pleasers, in contrast, tend to operate with a sense of transparency that encourages others in their orbit to do the same. In situations that mandate the type of compromise where no one is going to "get rich quick," Pleasers can often help strike a compromise where all parties live to fight another day.

One reason Pleasers are able to mediate conflicts so successfully is that they are able to tactfully address the emotional agendas on both sides. When tempers seethe, as they often do during conflicts, what people are able to articulate can't always encompass the passions that are driving them. Here's where a strong Pleaser often operates like a UN translator negotiating a peace accord. The Pleaser can objectively hear what opposing parties are disagreeing about at a logical level, such as the timing of a deadline or who is to blame for a work-related mistake. At the same time, the Pleaser is able to accurately spot the clues that reveal unspoken sensitivities, such as what each party is most fearful of and how each needs to be reassured to feel safe. This powerful capacity to be "bilingual" when dealing with thoughts and emotions comes from the instincts the Pleaser developed dealing with overextended parents.

Pleaser Blind Spots

While the Pleaser's capacity for empathy is one of their strongest gifts, their intuitive talents can also backfire on them. While the ability to fathom the unspoken agendas of others is a powerful skill, it can end up working against Pleasers who are more adept at reading others' needs than they are at standing up for their own.

Difficulty Advocating for Themselves

When Pleasers aren't clear about their own goals, they often find themselves so swept away by the drive to support others that they lose track of their own career plans. Bottom line: they are able to advocate for everyone *but* themselves. Remember, Pleasers were conditioned early in life to support others while asking little for themselves.

This blind spot can be costly for the Pleaser at any stage of career development. Managers, who are trained to keep costs low any way possible, can often spot a Pleaser a mile away. Some hiring managers have actually told me that they count on the fact that Pleasers will accept less compensation than their colleagues as long as they are promised that things will be better in the future. Until Pleasers become aware of the behavioral patterns that telegraph the ways that they are hardwired to seek approval and avoid conflict, they will remain at a disadvantage in salary negotiations.

The tendency to shy away from unpleasant topics also makes Pleasers easy to pass over for promotion. When several employees are vying for promotion, managers will often look for the person who is able to withstand the jealousy and backlash of their peers if they are asked to supervise them. Obviously, Pleasers don't stand out as the type of people who will whip a recalcitrant team into shape. This type of ability is more frequently associated with Commanders. What's worse, managers have told me that during a performance discussion, it's easier to placate a Pleaser, who will slink back to their desk thinking they just need to try harder, than it is to square off with a more aggressive employee who may demand a detailed explanation for why they were not advanced.

This blind spot doesn't disappear at the senior management level. Make no mistake about it—Pleasers can end up abruptly elevated to senior management positions, particularly when they have been the "people person" working behind the scenes, and the leader they have been supporting gets removed. Admittedly, by the time someone reaches CEO status, they have probably been able to draw on a diverse range of power styles when necessary and aren't operating exclusively in the Pleaser camp. That said, I've worked with a number of CEOs who self-identified as Pleasers. In dealing with a contentious board of directors, these Pleasers sometimes discover that their hesitation about advocating for themselves personally can undermine their ability to advocate for initiatives that are unpopular with their board.

In addition to career ramifications, the failure to advocate can also have an impact on job performance. While Pleasers may handle disgruntled clients with just the right touch, the tendency to acquiesce means they may give in too much to the clients and partners in negotiations and in other situations where the organization needs a firm stance.

Difficulty Standing Up to Bullies at Work

Lack of assertiveness with their peers is a common problem for Pleasers. Their distracted parents, less aware of the challenges their kids were facing, often didn't take the time to teach them how to "push back" on the playing field early in life. This can haunt the Pleaser on the job, when a bully starts stomping into his or her professional turf.

The highly diplomatic Pleaser is usually trying to deal with the facts so that everyone can strike a fair compromise. However, bullies often don't care about the facts and don't want to understand anything—they simply want what they want. With no coaching from parents on how to respond to raw aggression, Pleasers learn to adapt by withdrawing and staying off the radar screen of aggressive peers.

In a competitive work environment, the habit of avoiding conflict can be costly. Pleasers often learn the hard way that no matter how high their hard work has taken them in an organization, there are a myriad of professional situations where their peers will take them down a notch if they can't defend their position.

The Need for External Validation

As we'll see, the instincts of the Pleaser were forged in a climate of scarcity, and this type of atmosphere leaves many Pleasers feeling anxious and insecure. Thus, the dark side of the Pleaser's sensitivity is that they harbor a deep-seated fear that they will not be liked by others because they don't measure up. This pervasive sense of self-doubt drives many Pleasers to demand constant reassurance and validation. It can make them approval junkies.

Any addict is vulnerable to being manipulated by the need for his or her fix, and this craving can be glaring for the Pleaser. To the extent that they are driven by the need for external validation, Pleasers will constantly strive to prove their worth. Because their experience in the family system has conditioned them to strive for the approval of a preoccupied parent, this blind spot gets particularly ugly when the Pleaser is working for a superior who is emotionally stingy when it comes to expressing appreciation. As we will see in chapter 3, managing up can be a special challenge for the Pleaser.

In a protracted scenario, where the Pleaser begins to feel starved for attention, this hardworking employee may eventually come to the conclusion that negative attention is better than feeling invisible.

As one Pleaser told me, "I can handle almost anything you dump on me, but please don't ignore me. I'd rather be stabbed with scissors." Pleasers being driven by the darker aspects of their blind spots aren't above complaining aggressively about an unappreciative boss behind their backs as they thrash about for ways to get attention. When their need to be noticed starts to express itself in twisted ways and goes underground, Pleasers devolve from being the cultural glue that holds a team together into a covert force of dissent that can sabotage a system's morale.

Loyal to a Fault

Basically, Pleasers long to find a leader or a system that can "take care" of them by giving them the validation and security they craved, but never got, from their preoccupied caregivers. The Pleasers longing for "parental approval" can cause them to confuse loyalty to a particular leader with loyalty to an organization. It can also make them masters of denial. As Cooper's career illustrates, a Pleaser needs someone to please. Bernie Ebbers, the charismatic CEO of WorldCom, fulfilled the savior role for a legion of employees and shareholders willing to follow him more because he was a compelling individual than because he was a thoughtful strategist. Ironically, it was Cooper, one of Ebbers's earliest and most selfless followers, who put her life and career on the line to seek the truth when her gut told her that something was amiss at the top. As she took this courageous stand, Cooper started operating less and less as a classic Pleaser and began drawing on many of the strengths we associate with Inspirers on the Power Grid.

Pleasers need to take care that their loyalty isn't driving them to produce results for others at their own expense. With their noses pressed trustingly to the grindstone, Pleasers can be stunned when they are passed over for promotion by less diligent colleagues who played the politics more skillfully. When Pleasers neglect the big picture in terms of the outlook for their industry, they can find themselves dispassionately downsized from organizations that they have devoted the best years of their working lives to support. Pleasers must be mindful that their loyalty to their superiors and their organizations doesn't eclipse their loyalty to themselves.

Personalize Professional Criticism

In sharp contrast to Charmers, who tend to loathe being scrutinized by others, Pleasers often crave performance evaluations. This is because being evaluated by the boss meets a myriad of unspoken emotional needs for the Pleaser. First, they get the undivided attention of the boss for a few precious minutes. Second, the boss is talking about *them*. Third, the boss is forced to acknowledge and evaluate their contributions. In the Pleaser's mind, this often adds up to a foolproof recipe for getting a gold star.

However, the reality of a performance evaluation often teaches a Pleaser to be careful what they wish for. First, an overworked and preoccupied boss can be impatient and unwilling to spend time reassuring one of the troops while Rome is burning. This can make the tone of a performance evaluation feel less like the fireside chat the Pleaser was secretly longing for and more like being called to the principal's office. The tone of such a discussion can be particularly stark if the Pleaser happens to be reporting to a Commander. As many an overworked Commander boss has confessed to me, "If they are doing it right, I don't need to mention it. All I have time for is listing the areas where they need to improve."

Another thing that can catch the Pleaser off guard during performance reviews is the lack of formal recognition they receive for doing other people's work in addition to their own. I've worked with Pleasers who were stunned that their boss didn't acknowledge that they were not only doing their own work, but also completing tasks for colleagues who were neglecting key details or dropping the ball. When their performance evaluations are strictly based on official job descriptions and overlook the Pleasers' unofficial demonstrations of dedication, Pleasers I've worked with have expressed reactions ranging from disappointment to betrayal.

Finally, there's little that feels constructive about any type of criticism when the Pleaser is driven by the need for another's approval. When the Pleaser is in the grip of this blind spot, anything that isn't complimentary can feel like an attack. Obviously, this type of emotional distortion can prevent the Pleaser from taking in feedback that might improve his or her performance.

A Pleaser's Family Background

The balance of power between the parental figures in an ideal family system is assumed to create enough emotional and financial abundance to not only fulfill the two of them, but simultaneously nurture and fulfill the needs of the children in the system. Sadly, in our fast-paced and economically stressed world, this isn't always the case.

Scarcity issues are at the heart of family systems that foster a Pleaser. The family system of a Pleaser is frequently characterized by parents whose behavior signals to the young Pleaser that there is something else more important than they are. Thanks to the demands that our hectic culture makes on the most well-intentioned parents, almost anything that takes the parents' attention away from the child at emotionally critical moments can qualify. Whether it's a work-addicted parent who habitually misses bedtime or a caretaking parent focused on a sick family member or even parents so romantically enmeshed that the kids end up taking a back seat, the emotional impact on Pleasers is the same—they learn never to expect too much, but do everything they can to try to achieve that attention all the same.

Pleasers get initiated into adulthood early in life. Whether their parents realize it or not (and usually they don't), Pleasers often adapt by trying to emulate adult behavior in an attempt to merit the time and attention of their caregivers.

Jeffrey Arnett—a professor of human development and family studies at the University of Missouri—has studied young people emerging from their family systems into the wider world, and researched the question of what it means to *actually* be an adult. His research showed that few people consider the tasks that adults "do," such as holding down a job, getting married, or making major purchases, reliable indicators of adulthood. According to Arnett's findings, an adult is rather someone who has mastered the inner tasks of accepting responsibility and making independent decisions. The risk for Pleasers is that they devote so much energy early in life to "acting like" adults to court their parents' approval—"doing" the right things, rather than mastering the responsibility that comes along with them—that they don't learn to set the boundaries necessary to chart their own course.

Pleasers' attempts to "act like" an adult prematurely in life often trap them emotionally in a level of infantile terror. They grow up hungry for validation and are easily triggered by the withdrawal of approval. This anxiety presents itself on the job when Pleasers find themselves age regressing in the presence of authority figures or needing the approval of others more than they need to be honest with themselves.

The extent of a Pleaser's need for approval starts coming into sharper focus when they choose a school and, later, when they enter the workforce. Whatever their genuine desires might be, when it comes to the expensive and emotional process of actually picking a school and signing up for a major, the need for others' approval can frequently cause the Pleaser to pursue whatever course of study appears to keep others happy. Many Pleasers report sacrificing their earliest career dreams to attend the schools their parents wanted them to attend. Pleasers describe being discouraged from pursuing "risky" career paths by well-intentioned family members and friends who wanted them to put financial security first.

Depending on the specifics of their family dynamic, some Pleasers report a strong drive to be of service to others that is similar in many ways to the altruistic urges that motivate Inspirers early in life.

Because they have often been conditioned to nurture others, teenage Pleasers frequently report being drawn to the helping professions or environmental protection work. Pleasers often report dreams of becoming counselors, scientists, or even theologians, who are focused on awakening the humanity of those they touch. Other Pleasers, who grew up with parents who were preoccupied with financial stress, often confess that making money is their top priority. However, the financially driven Pleaser tends to be motivated by the desire to provide for others rather than by the Charmer's desire for personal gain or the Commander's need to keep score.

After graduation, many Pleasers report picking their first job based on gaining the approval of their friends or spouse. Once this pattern of seeking external validation takes hold, it tends to continue through the formative years of the Pleasers' career. For example, Pleasers often report making important career moves because their boss asked them to do so "for the good of the firm." The hidden cost of this pattern of having their personal desires eclipsed by others' goals begins to mount over time. One Pleaser, sharing a joke he had heard in a support group, told me, "I'm afraid that when I die that someone else's life is going to flash before my eyes."

An example of how this habit of placating others rather than listening to themselves can be costly for the Pleaser comes from Ted, a well-respected emergency room doctor who was suffering from what he described as a "midcareer crisis." When Ted was a young man, he wanted to go to film school. Ted's father, a successful doctor, urged Ted to go to the same medical school that he had attended. Ted told me wistfully, "My parents convinced me I'd need to be financially secure to support a family. When I tried to explain my dreams to my father, he told me that if I wanted him to finance my education, I'd need to go pre-med."

What Ted's father could not have foreseen twenty years ago were the changes that took place in the medical profession during the course of his son's career. Once insurance companies got into the game, not only was it less lucrative to be a doctor, but Ted ended up having to put in such long hours to keep his career on track that he believes his work schedule contributed to his divorce.

Single at age fifty, Ted is finally headed back to film school. The underlying lesson embedded in this type of story for the Pleaser is to beware of being so focused on getting validation and support from others, even well-intentioned family members, that you abdicate responsibility for your own destiny.

At the 1999 conference for Spirituality and Psychotherapy sponsored by the National Institute of Psychotherapies in New York, the brilliant psychiatrist Marion Woodman told the audience that, "If a child is treated as a performance machine, they unconsciously begin to treat themselves that way."[4] Reviewing my notes from the conference years later, I realized that Woodman's observation applies across the Power Grid: the family systems of both the Pleaser and the Commander inadvertently reinforce the message that a person's value hinges on his or her accomplishments. As a result of this subtle but pervasive message, both Pleasers and Commanders often view themselves as performers first and people second. But while Pleasers internalize the tendency to sacrifice their own needs to serve other individuals (particularly those above them), Commanders internalize the need to suppress their feelings so they can stay focused on advancing to the top of the system.

When we consider the professional ramifications of the way the Pleaser has been conditioned later in life, we see that people who identify with the Pleaser power style are particularly challenged when it comes to advocating for themselves with their boss or any authority figure on the job. The challenge for the Pleaser is to break out of the scarcity mind-set so that they learn to value themselves from within and balance their calling to support others with a commitment to achieving their own goals.

The Pleaser in Career Transition

The Pleaser's need for approval, and the underlying insecurity that drives this need, present special challenges during a job transition. Since many of them make important choices based on what others want them to do, Pleasers who haven't worked through their blind spots can risk losing sight of their own professional goals in the service of "rescuing" a floundering organization or attempting to follow a boss who doesn't officially have a position for them yet.

The first thing Pleasers in transition need to do is slow down and consider how they can use a transitional point in their careers as a chance to start focusing on what *they* want and need. I've seen Pleasers, eager to help others, make hasty decisions. They may jump into business with a buddy from college, offer to "audition" for organizations that want them to work for free, or even walk away from a promising career to help someone in need. Don't get me wrong. This kind of behavior can be commendable. However, the Pleaser needs to make sure that such decisions are being made thoughtfully and not in the service of running away from their responsibility to be true to themselves and their genuine talents. Pleasers who are so driven to seek the approval of others that they avoid taking the time for self-reflection risk feeling taken advantage of and resentful down the line.

Resentment is the number one energy drain for hardworking Pleasers who have fallen into the trap of giving more than they get on a consistent basis. Pleasers tend to be caught off guard in situations where, due to mismanagement above them in the chain of command, they find themselves abruptly terminated. Remember, the hardworking and loyal Pleaser has often been so focused on what their superior wanted that they weren't considering how the big picture might put their entire organization at risk.

As they rebound from professional setbacks, Pleasers need to do more than update their résumés. They need to deal with the feelings of betrayal associated with supporting an organization that failed to back them. They also need to work through any anger they may feel toward themselves if they have lost the proper balance between what they give to their jobs and what their jobs give to them. This emotional work must be tackled head-on so that Pleasers are not inadvertently conveying self-doubt and residual resentment as they strive to get their careers back on track.

The good news is that Pleasers who take the time to focus on their strengths and locate organizations that will respect their diligence and attention to detail are often hot commodities. In outplacement situations when I'm brought in to coach twenty to thirty people at a time, after an entire firm or department is eliminated, I have seen candidates with Pleaser qualities hired immediately, while people who exhibit characteristics indicative of other power styles, particularly overly confident Commanders, get passed over. This tends to mystify some onlookers, particularly when Pleasers are chosen over colleagues at the same salary level that have stronger references and track records. What was the Pleaser's secret? It's simple. Pleasers tend to be less threatening to potential colleagues.

All types on the grid can benefit from incorporating the strengths of the Pleaser power style in transitional situations. Charmers often stride proudly into interviews so focused on dazzling the person they are meeting with that they inadvertently intimidate potential colleagues. Commanders can come across as so hard-nosed that, even while their talents are evident, people who interview them aren't sure they want to grapple with these individuals' intensity on a daily basis. Finally, Inspirers can be so enthusiastic about their vision of how to improve a business situation that potential employers wonder whether these individuals can keep their feet on the ground and simply do what is asked of them. When the interview situation is viewed from this perspective, it's no wonder that the more humble and dedicated Pleaser often ends up winning the beauty pageant.

A Pleaser in Action

John, the CFO for an asset management firm, has been a hard worker all his life. John's father was a struggling artist who had fallen back on odd jobs to keep his family financially secure. His mother was an art dealer whose main focus in life was helping her husband realize his creative ambitions. Because his parents valued open-mindedness and creativity, John had many of the qualities we often associate with Inspirers. However, John's emotional memories of his childhood were most strongly imprinted by the sense of responsibility he felt to help take over household responsibilities that his parents were too preoccupied to handle. The eldest of five, John spent much of his childhood looking out for his younger siblings while his parents were largely preoccupied with finding the right platform for his father's creative efforts. The fact that John never seemed to get the attention he longed for, particularly from his father, combined with the sense of duty he internalized for "parenting" some of his siblings, caused him to identify most strongly with the power style of a Pleaser.

During John's childhood, he often overheard his parents say, "Thank goodness we don't have to worry about John! He's the smart one, and he can take care of himself." As expected, John made great grades, did well in school, and required little attention from his teachers or his parents.

Once John entered the workforce, he rose steadily up the ranks based on hard work and merit. His willingness to burn the midnight oil ensured that he was generally well liked professionally. Conditioned to support others, John kept his own needs as modest as possible and tried to avoid making waves.

Like many Pleasers, John was also a fabulous leader when it came to running one of the more tactical divisions of a large organization. In the no-nonsense world of financial accounting, John was a seasoned mentor who led by example. He worked long hours right alongside his protégés, caught errors less seasoned professionals often glossed over, and always expressed appreciation for the efforts of his team. The people in John's division loved working for him.

Unfortunately, like many Pleasers, John had never learned how to stand up to bullies. His natural Pleaser tendencies caused him to withdraw from overtly volatile situations where he himself was under attack.

When John's research into the firm's financial reporting practices prompted him to raise concerns that made some of his peers uncomfortable, several executive committee members turned the situation into a public showdown by raising their voices and questioning his credibility in front of the chairman. Rather than pushing back with self-confidence to protect his power base, John felt paralyzed by this public tongue-lashing. Like many Pleasers, John was nervous presenting to groups and preferred one-on-one meetings. Being criticized in front of this senior audience brought one of his greatest fears to life. John subsequently missed several days of work due to emotional stress.

As a Pleaser, John's need for approval was causing him to personalize the issue when his colleagues were not listening to him. In his mind, he kept recycling painful thoughts like, Why don't they respect me more? Nobody ever appreciates me. I feel like such a wimp. This torturous litany kept John stuck in his blind spot.

In truth, what was fueling the disrespectful pushback from some of his colleagues had very little to do with John. Some of his peers were kicking up a fuss because they were terrified that John's responsible and methodical research would uncover ways that they had misreported key investment positions. Like many bullies, they had learned early in life that if you can intimidate people, they will stop asking questions.

John turned to coaching to get guidance on how to navigate the treacherous emotional dynamics that were threatening his career. By reflecting on how his family system had conditioned him to respond to stress, John realized that he had fallen into the classic Pleaser blind spot of personalizing professional criticism. Once John started to realize that the way others were responding to his findings had more to do with their insecurities than with his delivery, he started to get back on track professionally.

Getting back on track involved getting his intuition out of the deep freeze. Like a deer caught in the headlights, John had simply panicked when the bullies on the executive committee had started to stampede. As he was able to get some perspective on the fear that gripped him when he felt publicly ridiculed, John got back in touch with the intuitive impulse that had originally alerted him that something at his firm wasn't right.

By studying the strengths of the Commander, John got ready to do battle at the next executive management meeting. By working on a succinct and unapologetic delivery for his argument, John was prepared not only to revisit this controversial issue but to comport himself in a manner that reflected his seniority as a CFO.

Subsequent events proved that John's intuition had been right on target. In the ensuing months, his concerns began to unearth a host of financial reporting discrepancies, and his firm was plunged into regulatory turmoil. As this drama unfolded, John's reputation for keen insight and tenacity helped him land a job as the CFO at a competitor that was committed to excellence in its reporting standards. His career is flourishing.

Conclusion

When it comes to leading laterally, the Pleaser is a natural. When resources are low and demands are high, their intuition and capacity to exert power through others enables Pleasers to motivate others without losing their capacity for empathy. Pleasers are the ones we count on to have the strength to keep caring when others shut down, reach out when others withdraw, and stay focused when others get distracted under pressure. Our business community needs Pleasers in order to function. They are the glue that holds a corporate culture together and keeps a mission on track.

What Pleasers must learn is how to balance is their dedication to supporting others with a commitment to being true to themselves—advocating for themselves, standing up for themselves, and believing in themselves. When Pleasers give too much of themselves away, nobody wins. Doing the self-reflective work necessary to clarify their genuine goals is crucial for Pleasers. As they learn to validate themselves from within, Pleasers are able to use their intuition to identify organizations that will respect their gifts and enable them to thrive.

CHAPTER THREE

Pleaser Power Plays

Most of us realize that success is a team sport. Pleasers go beyond believing this adage; they live by it. As Pleasers work their way up the professional ladder, many of them strive to bring out the best in their colleagues. Unfortunately, some Pleasers prove to be better at supporting others than at supporting themselves on the job. Until they understand the way that their family system may have conditioned them to look outside themselves for validation, Pleasers may be vulnerable to being "played" by Charmers and Commanders who dangle approval in front of them like a carrot on a stick.

In addition, Pleasers face a special challenge when it comes to managing up. Obviously, we all want to please the boss. Add this natural incentive to make your superior happy to the Pleaser's occasionally exaggerated need for approval, and you have a recipe for anxiety and insecurity. To hold their own, particularly with a critical superior, Pleasers must become mindful of areas where they need to respectfully disagree, take a stand, and speak up for themselves if they want their full range of professional talents to be appreciated. Pleasers who don't master these skills often pay the price of being passed over for promotion by peers who appear more confident to senior management.

We'll come to this challenge later; we'll start now with what happens when a Pleaser needs to manage down—an obvious test for someone who has a need to be liked beyond their need to take charge.

When the Pleaser Is the Boss

Pleasers often long to make love, not war. However, in managerial roles, the power reflexes of command are sometimes required. When put it charge, some Pleasers become anxious that they will not be liked if they take a stand to enforce their authority. This insecurity is rooted in the Pleaser's longing for the approval of a preoccupied caregiver early in life. To lead effectively, Pleasers must keep a few simple principles front of mind to make sure that their collaborative talents aren't undermined by their emotional insecurities.

Establish Clear Performance Standards and Enforce Discipline When These Are Not Met

Let's face it: if you're a Pleaser, the place where your emotions are going to wipe out your capacity for logic is any time you have to deal with conflict. And when you're a boss, conflict is going to rear its head when members of your team aren't performing at peak. Thus, you'd better figure out a way to strengthen your capacity to be objective when you need to deliver the uncomfortable message to one of your team that there are areas where they need to improve. What's more, if you are managing a Charmer or a Commander, you need to lay out the consequences that are associated with underperformance, or these employees may be feigning agreement on the outside while they are yawning on the inside.

This kind of preplanning is a must for the Pleaser boss. You must clarify what your performance standards are and how they are going to be measured in a manner that everyone can clearly understand.

You must also *make sure* that your employees understand how you are keeping score. Finally, you must accept that enforcing consequences when someone doesn't cut it, even when it's someone you like personally, is critical to the group's ability to understand that you mean business—whether you enjoy it or not.

Project an Image of Strength

Pleasers should never underestimate how critical image is to keeping their staff in line. I learned this lesson working with the CEO of a prominent *Fortune* 500 company who lost ground not only with his board but with employees throughout his organization because his dedication to being a "nice guy" wasn't giving them what they needed to feel hopeful in a contracting economy. While nobody wanted this chairman to be mean spirited, throughout the firm employees confessed that they longed for a "wartime" CEO who gave them a sense that someone decisive was at the helm. Pleasers need to realize that good intentions are necessary, but not sufficient, when it comes to leadership in an uncertain business climate.

To keep people on track, the boss must look confident, sound confident, and act confident as much as possible. Don't ask for your employees' approval; instead, clearly state your decisions once you are sure about them. Projecting an image of strength can be a strain for the Pleaser who often longs to let his or her hair down. Pleasers under fire must resist the urge to unburden themselves emotionally with their staff. Many employees, particularly Charmers and Commanders, see emotional vulnerability as a sign of weakness. Maintain a decisive image, and keep your reports busy with clearly defined assignments.

Embrace Pushback—It Means Your Staff Is Thinking

When the Pleaser's need for approval is particularly acute, they may unconsciously equate agreement with approval. When the Pleaser is the boss (and a Commander as well), he or she may mistakenly believe that when someone disagrees with them, it's because they don't support them. Pleasers who confess they feel this way admit it's illogical and counterproductive, when they consider their reactions objectively. This type of reaction undermines the Pleaser's ability to lead effectively.

If you are a Pleaser in charge, remember that it's not your staff's job to validate your seniority or your point of view. That validation must come from within. When members of your team push back on your point of view—rejoice! At least they aren't asleep at the wheel. If you genuinely agree with their concerns, incorporate them. If you disagree, let them know you've heard their reservations but you have decided to override them. When you learn to operate with clarity, confidence, and courtesy on a regular basis, you won't need people to agree with you to boost your self-confidence. What's more, you are likely to set a tone where your staff feels motivated to think more deeply and share more freely about their perspective on your shared business goals.

Don't Expect to Be "Friends" with Your Staff

To a certain extent, every type on the grid knows they need to please their boss to get ahead and tries to operate accordingly. That said, Pleasers, who sometimes have an exaggerated need to be validated, may be vulnerable to being manipulated by a subordinate who senses how to "game" their need for approval. We often see dramatic examples of this when a Pleaser is managing a Charmer. Charmers, who have mastered the arts of persuasion in preschool, are all too willing to spend time with a Pleaser boss to get what they want. However, in the same way they learned to manipulate an emotionally needy parent, Charmers will quickly intuit when the boss gets "hooked" on their approval and turn the tables sharply. This often results in a Pleaser boss dancing to the tune of an insubordinate report who has learned that he or she can get away with murder. Don't try to become pals with this type of report, don't indulge in lengthy personal conversations to clear up professional mishaps, and use praise sparingly.

Power Grid Case Study: A Pleaser Managing the Charmer

Bryan is a Pleaser who inherited his father's celebrated restaurant and resort. Bryan has recently hired Dave, a Charmer, to be his general manager.

During the first couple of months of their working relationship, Bryan's head was spinning from all the hard work and attention he was getting from Dave. It was the honeymoon period for a Pleaser managing down to a Charmer, and Bryan loved it. Dave worked long hours to get up to speed and arrived early in the morning to brainstorm with Bryan. Bryan was particularly flattered when Dave began sharing some of his personal life with him, trusting him with stories of his off-work hours. Bryan became comfortable enough himself that he talked about his personal life with Dave too.

To be an effective boss, you must be able to operate with enough formal power to get your employees to toe the line. The challenge for Pleasers is that they hope so much that their employees will like them personally that it can be a struggle for them to set the limits necessary to manage others effectively. While Bryan's father might have left him with a potentially prosperous business, he also left Bryan with a huge self-esteem issue because he had focused so much of his attention on that business rather than on his son when Bryan was a little boy.

The classic dynamic we see when an emotionally needy Pleaser is managing an entitled Charmer is a role reversal. Since Charmers can be quite ambitious, they will often go out of their way to please the boss so that they themselves can get ahead. Charmers may even resort to manipulation. If it takes unstructured personal chats, the Charmer will paste on their most sympathetic smile, show up, and listen to the best of their ability. Basically, in the beginning of the relationship, the

Charmer will try to fulfill the Pleaser's longing to be validated. This is precisely what Dave did with Bryan up until the moment it no longer suited his own needs. When Dave felt safe enough to stop "pretending" that he cared so much about the minutia in Bryan's world, things started changing.

As we'll see in chapter 4, the simple truth that Charmers learned from managing their caregivers is that once they get an authority figure hooked on their approval, it's simpler to get what they want from them. How does the Charmer know when someone is hooked? When that person starts to compliment them too often. The risk for the overtly positive Pleaser is obvious.

Once the Charmer senses the Pleaser is emotionally hooked, the romance stops and the role reversal begins. At this point, it's hard to tell who's the boss.

After a few months, Dave began getting moody, showing up late for work, and getting peevish over minor details. Because Bryan felt that he had bonded "so personally" with his general manager, Bryan found himself unable to take Dave to task.

If you are a Pleaser, know that most Charmers have been falsely empowered by an authority figure from their family system. This is because, in many cases, the Charmer was raised by caregivers who turned to them for emotional support and guidance. Thus, Charmers begin most relationships with an inflated view of themselves. Praise a Charmer too much, and they will start doing less and demanding more. Often, they will start demanding a raise, and if they really think they have the Pleaser hooked, they will sulk until they get it. Pleasers need to remember to use praise sparingly with Charmers and be prepared to enforce concrete consequences if they underperform.

Bryan needed to learn to practice some of the strengths we associate with the Commander to get this working relationship back on track. First, he needed to set some clear performance expectations for Dave. As he did this, he needed to consider the way that his need for personal attention had undermined his leadership. Second, he needed to have a no-nonsense chat with Dave to make sure that his expectations were clearly communicated and understood. Finally, he needed to establish consequences and be prepared to enforce these if Dave dropped the ball. Once Bryan started setting some clear limits, both for himself and for Dave, they were able to reestablish a positive working rapport.

When the Pleaser Is a Peer

Because they have an emotional trigger that drives them to seek the approval of others, Pleasers often abdicate their opinions in favor of those of their peers. However, if the Pleaser's peers begin to suspect that all it takes is a little raw aggression to push them aside, the workplace can begin to feel like the dodgeball field in no time. To maintain the respect of their peers, Pleasers need to embrace some life lessons that other types on the grid may already grasp.

Know Your Boundaries and Protect Your Turf

It's a simple lesson, and one most people learn playing "king of the hill" in preschool. Why is this one such a toughie for the Pleaser? Because many Pleasers didn't learn how to protect their turf on the playground. In fact, some of them never made it to the playground at all. Pleasers were often dashing home as kids, making sure they took care of whatever their caregivers were too preoccupied to deal with. The upside for the Pleaser is that these men and women don't snap under pressure; they maintain an even tone that keeps them out of hot water. The downside is that they often don't do *anything* when an aggressive colleague simply shoves them out of the way. It's not as if they had the benefit of involved parents who were emotionally coaching them on how to handle raw aggression.

On the job, the equivalent of playground shoving is the colleague you don't work for who treats you as if you do. Many Pleasers report that when a peer starts barking orders, they often find themselves rushing around obediently before they rationally realize what's going on. This can leave the Pleaser seething with resentment on the inside but without the tools to recognize what's wrong. Thus, if you are a Pleaser, make sure you know the boundaries of your job description before you get subtly (or not so subtly) subordinated. Use the rules of the system to protect your professional boundaries, and keep a written job description on hand at all times.

Prioritize Respect over Affection

When Pleasers are unaware of how their drive to form strong personal alliances differs from the priorities of other types on the grid, they may make the mistake of being overly solicitous, hoping their colleagues will return this behavior in kind. It seems like only yesterday that a lovely and brilliant young Pleaser in my coaching practice was struggling with investment banking colleagues who were playing head games with her by questioning her competence, staffing her on substandard deals, and making innuendos to senior management that she "wasn't that bright." In fact, the problem was that this young woman was a walking brain trust whose mere presence brought out the dysfunctional side of some of her insecure colleagues. One afternoon, she was blinking back the tears as she asked me, "Do you think they'll ever like me?" Answering her, I realized I was making a point I'd been repeating to many Pleasers when I found myself saying, "It doesn't matter if they like you. It matters that they respect you." (This woman, by the way, has gone on to become an investment banking superstar. Her clients *adore* her—and respect her.) Grasping this lesson can be tricky for the tender-hearted Pleaser who longs to make "friends" on the job. That said, this is one of those lessons the Pleaser is destined to learn at some point in their careers.

Negotiate Practical Issues First and Personal Reactions Second

Pleasers, who long to keep the peace, can get rattled when a colleague blows up at them under pressure. This is because, in their family systems, Pleasers were often conditioned to be nurturers. When someone's upset, the Pleaser wants to fix their feelings first and the problem second. When a Pleaser is working with a peer on the job, these priorities need to be reversed. To stay on track professionally, the Pleaser must learn to stay focused on resolving the professional issue at hand and mopping up any hurt feelings later. When the Pleaser can get his or her colleagues focused on what they can do practically in the present—meeting the deadline, correcting the mistake, saving the client, and so forth—that solution-oriented mind-set can sometimes serve to repair the hurt feelings at the same time.

Accept Conflict as Constructive

Pleasers, whose collaborative instincts are often the glue that holds a culture together, can tire easily when faced with conflict. They just want it to go away; they want people to "play nicely," and hope that if they bury their heads in the sand long enough, the problem will blow over and all will be forgotten. This attitude misses an important point. Sometimes, conflict can be extremely healthy for an individual and for an organization's development. Conflict signals passion. It's a sign that there are stakes worth playing for and that people are in the game. When approached in a healthy manner, it can even be fun. As Pleasers develop a more balanced power style, and cultivate the tools they need to embrace conflict constructively, they begin to learn that the ability to resolve conflict often creates powerful professional alliances among peers. Avoiding conflict can sometimes signal that you are avoiding engaging with a professional peer in a fully involved way.

Power Grid Case Study: Separating Personal Feelings from Professional Goals

Dave, one of the oldest directors in the information technology division of a large investment bank, is a Pleaser. He has been repeatedly passed over for promotion and has worked with the firm for over a decade. Paul, an Inspirer, is a new hire who comes to the firm from an Internet company.

Dave's challenge in working with Paul shows us that Pleasers may have to manage more than their workload as they deal with their peers. Sometimes they have to manage their envy.

Like many Inspirers, Paul exhibited a natural charisma that drew others to him from his first day on the job. When Jeff, their boss, began to gravitate Paul's way, Dave found that he was so overwhelmed with jealousy that it was getting difficult for him to concentrate on his work.

Dave's feelings began to really get the better of him one morning when Jeff strolled down their floor, passed his office, and lingered in Paul's doorway "just to chat." One thing that made this scene particularly hard for Dave to witness was that Paul seemed so maddeningly nonchalant about a scene that would have had Dave dizzy with happiness if it had happened to him.

While Dave was trying not to stare at Paul and Jeff through the glass wall of his office, he was secretly hoping that Jeff would notice how industrious he looked as he hovered over his computer. Instead, he heard peals of laughter as the two grinned over some shared joke. Dave began swallowing hard and racking his brain for topics that would work for lighthearted small talk if Jeff decided to make the rounds and come by to chat with *him*. While Paul was a classic Inspirer, taking popularity for granted, Dave, like many Pleasers, was obsessed with the popularity scorecard.

As envy got the best of him, Dave began using the office grapevine to spread innuendos that Paul was positioning himself with the boss at others' expense. The pain that Dave felt at being overlooked turned itself into this toxic strain of gossip. However, a few months later, when Dave discovered that Paul had complimented his work in a couple of memos to Jeff, Dave quickly backed off his smear campaign.

How exhausting to be Dave! If his colleagues suspected how he was torturing himself to get the boss's attention, they probably would have suggested he take a vacation and get some perspective—for everyone's sake.

The lesson for the insecure Pleaser is, the moment you get triggered to stab someone in the back is the moment when it's best to be direct. Dave's strongest move would have been to simply go to Paul, acknowledge how well he seemed to be fitting in with the boss, and to ask for feedback on how to get his best ideas across to Jeff more effectively. Unfortunately, employees who harbor hidden agendas aren't inclined to deal directly. This is why, to operate clearly and powerfully with their peers, Pleasers need to separate their personal longings from their professional goals.

When a Pleaser Is a Subordinate

Being direct and succinct can be challenging for Pleasers. The Pleaser often hopes that by chatting personally with his or her superior, a bond will form that will fulfill the Pleaser's longing for attention and approval from an authority figure. This type of emotional agenda frequently backfires. To get ahead and stay ahead, the Pleaser needs to stay focused on their professional responsibilities and seek validation for their work rather than their capacity for office socializing.

Make Sure Your Opinion Matters as Much as Your Output

When a Pleaser describes the hard work they did to create a report, and then goes on to say that they will not be included in the discussion when the report is reviewed, I consider this a person who needs a power upgrade. You want your superiors to value your subjective opinion as well as your analytic output. Don't give everything away at once. Ask leading questions when you present material so you encourage people to think about what you are presenting to them. Focus on establishing a sense of personal presence, as well as a reputation for factual reliability, when you share your work with others.

Learn When to Push Back

Pleasers, who are overly focused on seeking the approval of others, may miss crucial opportunities to point out things their boss may have overlooked. This is not only risky for their organization, it may cause their superior to draw a far darker conclusion than that the Pleaser is tongue-tied. When problems or overlooked information come to light later, and this is often the case, a frustrated superior may come to the erroneous conclusion that the Pleaser didn't say anything because they simply weren't all that bright. While it's always wise to be cautious about when and how one pushes back, particularly if the boss is a Charmer or a Commander, Pleasers must train themselves to speak up respectfully when they have a strong view. Pleasers who learn the art of when to articulate their intuitive hunches tend to be highly valued on the job.

Respect the Value of Your Superior's Time

In a competitive work environment, Pleasers need to remember that the boss may be constantly thinking of the value of time. If we take this one step further, it's likely that the boss is thinking that their time is more valuable than that of their subordinates. For example, if you are below them in the system's chain of command, the Commander feels your job is to serve them. In tactical terms, the Commander views a business hierarchy much like a military rank. Can you imagine a private lingering in the tent of a general before the battle, wanting to brainstorm with his or her superior officer about the next campaign? This is what it feels like to Commanders when one of their reports wants to kick ideas around with them. Wherever the Pleaser suspects his or her boss may fall on the Power Grid, it's important to know when to get to the point quickly and curb the desire to bond conversationally. Pleasers must be mindful of the value of their superior's time and watch for subtle cues that the time for "informal chatting" is over.

Stay Focused on Professional Priorities

Many Pleasers slave away in the hopes that they will get the validation on the job that always seemed to elude them in their family systems. The flaw in this strategy for the Pleaser is that if the firm is going through a crisis or the boss happens to be a Charmer or a Commander, they're going to be waiting a long time for a compliment. Let's face it: managers are trained to focus primarily on one thing—the commercial point. While it often appears on the surface that Pleasers are focused on the organization's mission, motives may be lurking at a deeper level that can sabotage the relationship between a Pleaser and his or her boss. For example, when an Inspirer is the boss, basking in the glow of such an altruistic superior can get addictive for the emotionally hungry Pleaser. Bosses from any quadrant on the grid will eventually get burned out if the Pleaser needs too much "me time" with them. Thus, as Pleasers become more aware of how their need for attention can drive their behavior, they need to monitor the amount of time and attention they request from their superior.

Power Grid Case Study: When a Pleaser Meets His Commander Boss

Andy is a Pleaser who works as an engineer for a large aircraft manufacturer. His new boss, Steven, a Commander, was a recent hire brought on from one of their competitors to help them work on securing an important military contract.

Andy grew up in a farming community in rural Pennsylvania. His father worked repairing large machinery, and his mother helped run a local bakery. One of five children from a loving but financially strapped family, Andy learned to look out for himself early in life. One of the ways he did this was to make sure he knew what was going on with the people he worked with personally as well as professionally. Andy was a really friendly guy.

Andy's misguided attempt to make a good first impression with his boss shows us how the Pleaser's dream of bonding with authority can sometimes be a dangerous fantasy.

Andy approached Steven on his first day at the new firm for an informal chat about what was going on in their division. This seemed like a good idea to Andy because, after all, this is what any Pleaser would have welcomed from a new team member.

Andy was surprised and stung by the terse and unwelcoming manner in which Steven looked up and greeted him with a demanding "Yes?" when he saw Andy standing in his doorway. A Pleaser who was easily hurt by being rebuffed, Andy stood like a deer in the headlights for a few uncomfortable moments and fumbled to explain why he had decided to just "drop by." He thought he had been coming by to earn a few points with his new supervisor—and instead he was losing ground as the seconds ticked by.

Here's a clear example of how the Pleaser and the Commander can see the same situation very differently. From Andy's point of view as a Pleaser, an informal chat gave colleagues that important moment to bond personally. For a Pleaser longing for attention, this is what the heart and soul of business is about.

While a Commander presents a dramatic example, a boss from any quadrant on the grid finding a new employee in the doorway may sense a dilemma. For example, a new boss may hope to establish discipline among new reports in order to keep them focused on the job.

If this is the case, the boss may wonder how he or she will be able to make a department run successfully if the employees feel free to wander in with idle chitchat.

While Andy's situation looks grim on the surface, it's important to bear in mind that Pleasers can have fabulous careers reporting to Commanders as long as they remember what to focus on when they interact with this type of boss. In Andy's case, it's helpful to remember that Commanders can be structure junkies. In other words, they never met a rule they didn't like. As we know, Pleasers are great with details. Thus, one way a Pleaser can win the heart of a Commander is by becoming an expert on the rule book. Regardless of the quadrant the boss falls in, Pleasers will be headed in the right direction when they turn their laserlike focus on the details their superiors care about rather than longing for more face time.

Conclusion

Self-confident Pleasers rise to the top. This is because once they have learned to trust their intuition under pressure, Pleasers are able to balance a keen eye for business detail with a keen sense of what motivates others in a way that can take their colleagues' breath away.

Pleasers who have learned to "kick the habit" when it comes to their addiction for approval still approach their careers with an innate tendency to support others. What they have learned is how to do this without sacrificing themselves in the process. This makes them leaders who can envision and execute business solutions that are profitable for their cultures and their cash flow simultaneously.

CHAPTER FOUR

Meet the Charmer

The acid test of anyone's professional reputation is often what others say about them behind their backs. "I don't know how he (or she) *does* it!" is a refrain we often hear when people are describing a Charmer. Whether they have managed to land a client no one else in the firm could close, come from behind to get a coveted promotion, or even get their start-up company on the radar screen of big investors, an aura of intimidating mystery surrounds Charmers. It's not just how often they win the game that fascinates us, it's that they have an uncanny ability to redefine the rules of the game to suit themselves that leaves other types on the grid shaking their heads in wonder.

Because the emotional intensity that Charmers exude compels our attention, participants in our workshops often cite celebrities when discussing people who exhibit this power style. Sports celebrity Darryl Strawberry is one of the people frequently mentioned as exemplifying the power style of a Charmer. Other Charmers noted as much for their personal drama as their professional success include Angelina Jolie, Ivan Boesky, and Frank Sinatra.

Approximately 25 percent of the people sent to us for coaching from

Fortune 500 companies consider themselves Charmers. These individuals are often highly successful rainmakers in their organizations.

Strengths of the Charmer

As we shall see, Charmers tend to be consummate strategists who get what they want—even when the odds appear to be against them. They are determined, influential, and powerful change agents.

Charmers Have a Keen Sense of How to Influence Others

We don't call them "Charmers" for nothing. Many Charmers became masters of persuasion early in their childhoods. The creative methods Charmers use to impress their superiors can make Pleasers and Commanders envious. This is because Pleasers and Commanders, who have been conditioned to know their place in the pecking order and stay there, simply don't feel entitled to the attention of those in charge the way Charmers do. That said, when the Charmer manages to land a golf date with the boss or get the firm's top client to meet them for lunch, such bold moves often spark widespread admiration. Who hasn't read *The Prince* by Machiavelli (the überCharmer) and fantasized about being an expert at the art of influence?

Starting early in childhood, where they often learned how to play one parent against the other, Charmers have cultivated the art of using private interactions to get what they want. Sadly, young Charmers often feel forced to become consummate strategists early-on to survive emotionally.

Later in life, people who have been conditioned to operate as Charmers often have an uncanny ability to seduce their superiors, and sometimes even their clients, into giving them what they want. Whether it's conscious or unconscious, Charmers are able to get the boss to think of them as the heir apparent they always longed for, or an important client to feel like their "best friend." Their talent for fostering the illusion of a "special" emotional connection with people in charge gives Charmers the power to close deals and get promotions that can elude Pleasers and Commanders.

Charmers Can Produce Results in Whatever Incentive System You Create

No matter how complex the maze, Charmers have power genes that compel them to find the cheese, find it first, and run off with the biggest hunk they can carry. Put them on commission, and they will close deals on a scale you couldn't have imagined possible. Take away their commission, and they will find a way to get promoted to a position where they can grab a chunk of equity in the firm. While they may not always have the most formal authority in their organizations, they tend to take home the largest paychecks.

Whatever the industry and however compensation is decided, Charmers are notoriously successful rainmakers. This is because they are able to balance a keen insight into what sways others emotionally with their own logical detachment. While the Pleaser is attuned to the needs of others on the job, often at their own expense, the Charmer is able to keep their own interests in mind while hitting it out of the park for their organizations.

In the business of professional sports, Darryl Strawberry's rapport with the crowd kept fans buying tickets for years. In his popular autobiography, *Straw: Finding My Way,* Strawberry describes how his instincts around what would pack stadiums helped him rise to the top in the competitive world of pro baseball: "Go up to bat, they're booing—*pow.* Hit my first one off the scoreboard. The place erupts. Now they're all up on their feet cheering. I go around the bases all nonchalant, like I don't even hear them. Get back into the dugout, and instead of coming out for a curtain call, I go down the tunnel for a smoke. You were booing me a minute ago, now you want me to come out? Nuh-uh . . . Next time I come out to bat they're like statues all around the park. They have to pee . . . they hold it . . . *Boom,* I slam another one over the left field wall. The place erupts."[1]

Whether they're working in the theater or on a trading floor, Charmers have a natural instinct for keeping one eye on what drives revenue and the other eye on what fuels passion. They also tend to be keenly aware of the value they are bringing to those around them. Thus, while Charmers can be challenging to manage, they are often well worth the effort.

Charmers Are Master Problem Solvers

Charmers are strategic thinkers to the core. If you have a business problem you can't solve, look for a Charmer. Their dispassionate ability to analyze situations can cut through the most tangled web of professional intrigue. What's more, if you have a new idea for a business venture, you definitely want to run it past a Charmer before you put too many resources behind executing it. While the Charmer's ability to become clinically unsentimental about the prospects for a business venture can be chilling, their thought process tends to be so thorough that it's worth the drop in temperature.

Any member of management who has had the pleasure of being raked over the coals in a meeting by a talented Charmer in sales can testify to this. Whether they are working in the private sector or even as political operatives, Charmers can often tell you bluntly what will or won't sell—and why. What's more, they are often right. That's why having some talented Charmers on your team can be critical to your firm's success. Remember, if you can get your idea past a Charmer, you can probably sell it to anyone.

Charmers Can Be Powerful Change Agents

Your basic Charmer simply won't believe what authority figures tell them "just because they said so." Charmers question almost everything.

They question authority. They question rules and structure. They question prevailing beliefs. Granted, this widespread questioning is often in pursuit of their own goals, but smart organizations recognize the larger potential in the Charmer's questions.

The Charmer's penchant for independent thinking stems from the fact that, in early childhood, he or she may have experienced a role reversal and felt the need to hold a caregiver accountable for immature behavior. One Charmer told me he tried to keep his mother's checkbook in order for her, and another told me she used to hide her father's cigarettes so he wouldn't smoke himself to death. In the opening of his autobiography, Darryl Strawberry writes about having to restrain his alcoholic father to protect his mother.

While this type of role reversal is dysfunctional in many ways, an upside is that it empowers Charmers to address problems that Pleasers and Commanders may turn a blind eye to or overlook. This is because Pleasers and Commanders are less likely to question authority. The Pleaser is usually too busy trying to win the approval of those in charge to question the way the overall hierarchy functions, and the Commander is usually too busy trying to advance within the system to question the system itself. While Inspirers are willing to question the top brass, they are also predisposed to leave systems that don't reflect their values rather than fighting to advance within them. Thus, without Charmers in our organizations, we would rarely have the change agents necessary to question what's going on with a system when it has lost its way.

Frank Sinatra, who spent much of his childhood learning to grapple with both his short-tempered mother and the violent kids on the New Jersey streets, grew up to become a powerful Charmer and change agent in the entertainment industry. In an article for the *Nation*, journalist Jon Wiener chronicled the high price Sinatra paid for defending liberal ideas, such as racial integration, early in his career. Wiener writes, "The pundits called it "Frank's big nosedive . . . Columbia records asked Sinatra to give back his advance, MGM released him from his film contract, he was fired from his radio show and his agent dropped him. His career, like those of so many other victims of Mc-Carthyism, was in ruins."[2]

But never underestimate a Charmer's ability to recover from a setback. Sinatra's comeback in the entertainment industry was with his 1953 hit film *From Here to Eternity.* He also went on to return to politics as a Democrat. Frank Sinatra, like many powerful change agents, was someone who was going to make up his own mind about the "rules" rather than blindly obeying them.

Charmer Blind Spots

The Charmer's drive is a double-edged sword. While their ambition fuels their rise to the top, this same determination can trip them up at critical moments in their careers. This is because the Charmer's race for success is propelled by more than a zeal for outer accomplishments. They often dash from one achievement to the next because they are compelled by the need to distract themselves from uncomfortable feelings within.

Charmers Are Focused on Results—Not Process

This blind spot highlights one of the main ways in which Charmers differ from Pleasers. Pleasers, who are sensitive to others' feelings, are all about the process and getting the best out of people while they get to the desired outcome. In contrast, Charmers apply their brainpower to the problem at hand and to producing results anyway they can.

As we'll see, thanks to the survival skills they developed in childhood, Charmers don't wait for instructions and road maps. Once they know what the goal is, they will map out what they think is the most efficient route and get moving. If they violate the process along the way, they'll consider apologizing later. After they collect their bonus.

Ivan Boesky was a prominent figure on Wall Street whose flamboyant lifestyle and well-publicized philanthropy kept him in the headlines in the 1980s. Boesky's relentless drive to achieve, combined with the stormy dynamics in his personal life, has prompted many of our participants to cite him as an example of a Charmer.

Boesky went from famous to infamous when he began bending the rules too far by using insider tips to make huge stock trades only a few days before the corporation he was trading announced a takeover. This practice caused the SEC to crack down on insider trading, and was so widely publicized in the 1980s that, well over a decade later, Brad Pitt's character in the film *Ocean's Eleven* referred to a confidence scheme involving insider information as a "Boesky."

In their article on Boesky for *Time* magazine, journalists Stephen Koepp, Bill Johnson, and Frederick Ungeheur wrote, "No amount of money seemed to convince [Boesky] that he had finally arrived . . . He seemed determined to become richer than his father-in-law. His zealousness shocked the arbitrage business, which had become accustomed to small, cautious investments. Boesky frequently bet the ranch on single takeover bids."[3]

In describing the types of trades Boesky pioneered, which took an unwary Wall Street by storm, these journalists were chronicling a Charmer who was inventing his own rules faster than his industry could regulate him. While few Charmers bend the rules so far that they break, Boesky serves as a reminder of what can happen when the drive to excel becomes so excessive that it eventually sows the seeds of a business leader's demise.

Charmers Have a Tendency to Overextend Themselves

Charmers are so driven to best their colleagues and produce superior results that many of them will go to extremes to avoid looking within to analyze why they run as hard as they do. As we have noted, the fear that keeps some Charmers frantically avoiding feelings stems from their inability to trust one or both of their primary caregivers.

There's a huge downside to being compulsively driven that can put the organizations that Charmers work for at risk. Charmers may create big, complex deals and start juggling way too many balls at once in an effort to accelerate their momentum. If they haven't taken the time to create real collaborative relationships that will sustain them during the inevitable ups and downs of a tumultuous business environment, things can get messy and extremely expensive if the wrong balls hit the ground.

One Charmer told me that, in his opinion, "great salespeople never stop selling." Charmers with this attitude often end up juggling so many balls that the line between their professional obligations and their personal life blurs. One Charmer I worked with, who was one of the most successful salespeople at her hedge fund, was constantly flying around the world to network with clients, throwing dinner parties to support her husband's political career, and adopting multiple children to try to build the kind of caring family she never had as a child. The problem was that she had so much on her plate that she was rarely fully present for any of it. In our early coaching sessions, she would often burst into tears from the sheer physical exhaustion of keeping her image up in all facets of her life.

In his autobiography, Darryl Strawberry writes about not only the professional risks he exposed his sports franchise to, but the high personal cost he paid for overextending himself. His life changed dramatically when he became the number one draft pick in the nation his senior year in high school. While life looked like a fantasy on the outside, Strawberry was still unable to trust himself on the inside. Like many Charmers, he began to live a double life. In the sports industry, he was a revenue-producing asset to his franchise. On the inside, he was in full flight from the childhood trauma of battling with an abusive, alcoholic father. In extreme cases, the Charmers' flight from disowned feelings can make them so focused on personal gain that their professional judgment becomes impaired. For Strawberry, who had a proclivity to indulge in drugs and dangerous behavior, this inner flight cost him much more than his baseball career—it came close to costing him his life.

Charmers Tend to Isolate Themselves

Because the risks they take are often larger than they'd even like to admit to themselves, Charmers may isolate themselves so they won't be drawn into conversations that would require them to disclose *how* they go about producing the results that take them to the top. They rationalize taking big risks because many of them honestly believe they are smarter than the people they work for. After all, if you've convinced yourself that you are smarter than your parents as a child, how hard is it to believe later that you are smarter than your manager?

Many Charmers have learned to have more faith in their own judgment than they did in their caregivers. Later in life, these Charmers may become conditioned to value their own intellect and opinion over the advice of their managers and/or the prevailing wisdom of their group. This attitude reinforces the Charmer's tendency to operate as a lone wolf.

When they isolate themselves, Charmers may miss vital feedback from others that would clue them in that their behavior has led them into the danger zone. When the Charmer loses perspective in terms of how his or her behavior is being experienced by others in the system, the Pleasers and Commanders who may have been watching the Charmer's ascent from the sidelines often take a step back and wait for the Charmer to self-destruct. Less benevolent colleagues may even try to help this process along.

Charmers See Emotional Vulnerability as a Weakness

Charmers are not flawed people, but they often operate with a flawed framework. Self-disclosure and soul-searching are challenging for the

Charmer, because their childhood has made it difficult for them to feel emotionally safe in the presence of others.

Nobody fears being manipulated more than a master manipulator. Because of this, Charmers have difficulty trusting others, and when others sense this, they have difficulty trusting the Charmer in return. These trust issues are at the heart of why, in spite of their strategic talents, Charmers can sometimes find it difficult to achieve and maintain leadership positions in large organizations.

An example that illustrates this blind spot comes from a talented South Korean Charmer we worked with, Yoon, who did everything he could think of to establish himself as the pipeline to Asian wealth in the minds of his American firm's board of directors. His blind spot came into play when he avoided discussing his plans with his subordinates and adopted a cold and withdrawn management style so that he wouldn't be emotionally swayed by the American "cowboys" who reported to him.

When the board decided it was time to do some reshuffling at the senior management level, Yoon was delighted to discover that he was being considered as a successor for the firm's current president. His hard work was finally paying off! Yoon longed for the public recognition that came with this type of high-profile position.

Sadly for him, when the grapevine got the news that the board was looking for a new president, top producers throughout the organization threatened to leave if Yoon was seriously considered for this post. It turned out that Yoon was only able to create his impressive revenue numbers by strategically downsizing and ruthlessly managing his department. Because he was so hesitant to allow his direct reports to have any influence over him, he went to the other extreme and treated them more like chess pieces than people. While he had been making money (at least on paper), he had been making enemies as well. His strategy backfired, and he not only got passed over for the top slot, he subsequently left the firm.

The inner world of Charmers is a complex place where they are anxiously sifting through the motives and skills of others to make sure they have mapped out the best strategy for themselves before they get manipulated by someone else. While they are largely driven by fear and have trouble trusting others, this in no way means they are bad people. They simply see life, and business, as a game where if they don't win—they lose.

What's more, like all of us, Charmers long to be liked. Don't let a Charmer with an intimidating image fool you. They may seem unconcerned with what others think of them, but behind closed doors Charmers will brood over a perceived slight, fret about their image, and often become highly sentimental over seemingly trivial events. My work has taught me that the more intimidating the Charmer's outer shell is, the more likely they are to be protecting a sensitive inner core.

A Charmer's Family Background

A classic Charmer is a lone wolf who has often been raised in a system where people operate behind each other's backs effortlessly, elegantly, and automatically. It's second nature for them to triangulate. This back-door approach to amassing power is the result of a breakdown in the formal authority structure of the family system. Ideally, the authority figures in a family system are role models who support each other and provide a united front when it comes to power struggles with and among the children. However, for Charmers, it's never been that simple. Due to divorce, parental illness, or simply the kind of emotional estrangement that weakens a marital bond rather than breaking it, the Charmer has learned that when parental authority is inconsistent, it can't always be trusted.

Gerald Gardner, a clinical professor of child psychiatry at Columbia University, coined the term *Parental Alienation Syndrome* (PAS). In essence, PAS is a term Gardner developed to describe the destructive impact on a child of one parent's alienation from the other. According to Gardner, the risk to the child of developing adult depression or a manipulative style of interpersonal behavior later in life intensifies to the degree that the child becomes a pawn in the rift between the parents.

Amy Baker, author of *Adult Children of Parental Alienation Syndrome: Breaking the Ties That Bind,* describes how seeking "adult" support from one's children can distort the parenting process: "When children feel that their parents are more like friends than like parents, it may indicate that the alienating parent is sharing too much information with the child, is relying on the child for support and comfort, and may not be setting appropriate limits."[4]

A lively debate is under way among mental health professionals as to whether PAS qualifies for inclusion in the *Diagnostic and Statistical Manual of Mental Disorders.* What is not in question, however, is that almost all the Charmers I have worked with report an intense emotional entanglement with one of their caregivers. Some Charmers have described feeling as if they had to serve as a therapist for one of their parents. Others report being treated like a spousal substitute for an angry or alienated caregiver.

An ongoing need to emotionally soothe a troubled caregiver gradually erodes the child's respect for formal authority. This lack of respect for authority is the foundation of the trust issues that emerge later in life when the Charmer enters the workforce. After all, since consistency and supportive behavior were never modeled for Charmers, they have come to the sad conclusion that many people are only out for themselves. Why shouldn't they operate that way?

As happens with many Charmers, Darryl Strawberry's trust issues with his father manifested in difficulty respecting authority figures in general. While he had already fallen into a pattern of violence and substance abuse by high school, Strawberry found a refuge in sports. He notes that his early coaches had their hands full with him because, as with many Charmers, his ego convinced him that he didn't need anyone. That said, Strawberry gained some structure in his early years from a couple of coaches who refused to let him play when he was disrespectful or undisciplined.

When Charmers leave home and begin to establish an identity outside their family system, the survival skills that they developed to emotionally support a troubled parent tend to blossom into seductive talents. When this happens, Charmers begin to develop a taste for conditioning others to comply with them. Whether their strengths are intellectual, social, or even physical, once Charmers feel the rush of power over others—they want more.

Charmers tend to select their college and their major based on the reputation that these campuses and courses have for putting them on the "fast track" to wealth and power. They will look for schools that have a reputation for getting graduates into top firms, training students in cutting-edge technology, and attracting faculty with celebrity status.

Once Charmers start considering the job market, they tend to look for a work environment where they will be promoted fast and make as much money as possible. As a result, Charmers are often drawn to commission-driven jobs that status-conscious Commanders may view as too risky—as long as the payment system is clear to them. This is because, ironically, the Charmer isn't as worried about financial security as people from other quadrants tend to be (the Charmer learned early in the game that nothing in life is too secure).

The Charmer in Transition

Job transitions often produce less anxiety for Charmers than they do for Pleasers and Commanders because, deep down, Charmers know that they have an edge when it comes to selling themselves. What's more, since they have a tendency to always be on the lookout for a bigger and better deal, Charmers often have a list of fallback opportunities lined up long before they need them.

What Charmers have to bear in mind is the well-known adage "Be careful what you wish for." Because they are consummate spin doctors, Charmers need to make sure that they don't oversell themselves in the interview process.

Thanks to their impressive management skills, some Charmers are able to enthrall prospective employers who hire them on the spot for positions they aren't fully qualified to perform. This rarely ends well. Once Charmers have been promoted beyond their skill level, they tend to focus on hiding their shortcomings rather than on accessing the training and feedback they need to rise to the challenge responsibly.

Edward, a frightened and sleep-deprived Charmer, confessed a tale of woe after an interview that went far better than it should have. A handsome young graduate from Oxford, Edward had been hired to manage money for a growing hedge fund. The only problem was that Edward knew virtually nothing about running money. He couldn't even distinguish between value and growth as investment styles.

When I asked him how he secured the job, Edward explained that he had charmed the head of the firm into thinking of him as the son he never had. Unfortunately, since Edward was hesitant to admit what he didn't know, he needed to quickly get the training required to do his job responsibly, or he risked losing a great deal of money for investors.

Most Charmers know their stuff. Before we write Edward off as a fraud, it's important to bear in mind that there were some pretty important things he *did* know that landed him a job he was functionally unprepared for. For one thing, Edward knew what names to drop. What's more, when things went better in his interview than he expected, Edward quickly realized what he needed to learn, and worked frantically to do so.

The lesson here for employers is to realize that the "rosy glow" they feel in an interview may not be their intuition telling them they've found the right candidate. That glow may be the rush that comes from the seductive tractor beam of a Charmer. On the other side of the desk, for the sake of their professional reputations, Charmers must be realistic about what they are willing to and able to provide a prospective employer.

A Charmer in Action

Amy is a Charmer who didn't realize that her ambition was driven as much by a flight from her repressed feelings as by a genuine commitment to her work. What's particularly compelling about Amy's story is that it illustrates the way that, with guidance, Charmers can draw on their formidable capacity for control in order to manage their own ineffective behavior. Once Amy took the time to look within, she was able to channel the energy she had previously used to run away from her feelings into repairing key professional relationships.

Amy, a managing director in investment banking, is a high-energy go-getter who is absolutely charming to her higher-ups—and to anyone she thinks can get her something that she wants.

Amy's experience in her family system left her with deep-seated trust issues. When Amy was a small child, her presence actually helped the family pull together. However, two things changed around the time that she became a teenager. Her father, John, who ran his own architectural firm, ended up working long hours when his firm fell on troubled times, and he wasn't able to be home much of the time. Her mother, Sally, was an alcoholic who acted like a spoiled child when she was drunk.

Sally couldn't bear sharing her husband with anyone—even her daughter. To make sure she was the center of attention, Sally began "inventing" things that Amy had done wrong, to monopolize her husband's attention once he finally made it home. By driving a wedge between John and Amy, Sally managed to prevent him from doting too much on his daughter. These tragic incidents not only destroyed Amy's faith in both her parents but, by extension, left her mistrustful of women in general.

When Amy finally got away to college, she emerged as a beautiful and charming, but very angry, young woman. Because she had felt so emotionally out of control as a child, Amy learned to control everything she could as a young woman, hoping she would finally feel safe. She obsessed about her grades and made top marks in her class. She controlled her peers and became somebody no one wanted to cross. To take control of her future, Amy did everything she could think of to become one of the most sought-after job candidates to graduate from her university.

Once she landed a good job on Wall Street, Amy never looked back. Her career was everything to her. When she decided she needed a partner to help her network her way to the top, she quickly met and married Nathan. Nathan was a docile young man who worked long hours as a chef and let Amy call most of the shots on the home front. He kept her fed; she kept him financed. Unfortunately, neither one of them put too much emotional effort into the marriage.

Like many Charmers, Amy put most of her energy into impressing management on the job. She was so focused on her male bosses that she could tell you where they liked to dine, what they did for recreation, and even what their favorite colors were. In contrast, one year she actually forgot her husband's birthday.

When the senior managers at her firm began to show an interest in funding a diversity program, Amy seized the opportunity to be in the limelight as a point person. She convinced them that she should run the women's network, and used the position to get face time with as many influential leaders as possible. The problem was that Amy could honestly not have cared any less about supporting other women. Her primary goal was to showcase herself.

There were a few subtle signs along the way that Amy's interest in the women's initiative wasn't totally altruistic. For example, she tended to impatiently brush past young women eager to speak with her at public events, particularly when she spotted a senior male entering the room. She also dodged calls from young women on their way up the career ladder and tended to only meet with business celebrities. However, even though her track record as a mentor was spotty, she'd been so successful at getting senior management to fund lavish dinners and networking events that nobody was complaining.

People who work alongside Charmers can find them to be capricious and impulsive, and Amy was no exception. It was tough to fault her work because her clients loved her and she produced a spectacular revenue stream for the firm. The people who worked alongside her, however, were occasionally in for a bumpy ride. Sometimes she was preternaturally insightful and supported her peers. Other times, with little warning, the storm clouds would gather in Amy's inner world, and she would become vindictive and judgmental over some imagined slight. Her colleagues often complained that they never knew whether they would be dealing with the superstar or the spoiled child.

Charmers are often plagued with unresolved feelings because they were never really able to be children emotionally during childhood. One Charmer actually told me that he felt he was born a "short adult." Thus, the suppressed emotions often simmer just beneath the surface of the Charmer's carefully crafted professional image. These hidden feelings, which many Charmers strive to suppress through achievement and nonstop business, can bubble up unexpectedly whenever the Charmer feels threatened.

Amy felt threatened the day she found out that her firm was hiring Cindy, an investment banker with a successful track record, from one of their key competitors. Since Amy was the most senior woman in the division, and Cindy was being groomed to be a rising star, it seemed natural for Amy to mentor her. After all, Amy was devoted to supporting the careers of other women, right?

Amy, who genuinely wanted to be liked and to get ahead, was blindsided when Cindy's presence began to trigger the buried rage she felt toward women that stemmed from her history with her mother. Amy had repressed these powerful feelings so deeply that even she was unaware of them.

While Amy was smiling on the surface when she and Cindy were in meetings together, she was seething underneath. Everything Cindy did seemed to enrage Amy, whose internal dialogue was firing off statements like, If she thinks she's going to outshine *me*, she's got another think coming!

Amy found herself on the hot seat fast when her resentful feelings began to overshadow her professionalism. Things came to a head after an important marketing meeting, when the client called her boss and told him that Amy's passive-aggressive demeanor toward Cindy had made him uncomfortable.

The reaction to this incident was so strong that it made Amy's head spin. Her boss not only called her on the carpet privately, he insisted that she formally apologize to the client and to Cindy. He also told her that Cindy would be replacing her as the head of the firm's diversity committee in the coming year. Clearly, by putting Cindy in her crosshairs, Amy had picked the wrong target.

Finding herself in a professional nosedive, Amy hired a coach to help her figure out what had gone wrong.

The first thing Amy had to do was slow down. The suppressed emotional intensity that fuels the ambition of Charmers sometimes drives them to rush nonstop from accomplishment to accomplishment. Obsessed with their current goal, they don't take the time to reflect. As she began to make room for self-reflective work, Amy realized that she had come a long way in life without acknowledging and understanding that her ambition was fueled by disowned anger.

In part by studying the power styles of other types on the grid, Amy was also able to learn new tools to help her rebuild her strained relationships with colleagues. The more she learned about Pleasers, the more horrified Amy was to realize that, on a bad day, she would blow off steam at the expense of her subordinates. While she had also proved to be a supportive mentor to employees she felt showed genuine promise, Amy's emotional inconsistency had left many members of her team feeling off balance. Amy was relieved to find that once she started expressing more consistent appreciation toward her group and practicing patience under pressure, most of her staff were more than willing to support her.

Reflecting on the power style of the Inspirer gave Amy a more sincere appreciation for the importance of her firm's diversity program. The old Amy would have simply dropped all involvement in this initiative if it wasn't going to get her "extra credit" with senior managers. Amy surprised everyone when she volunteered to work on several committees behind the scenes to support women's advancement in the firm, even though Cindy had replaced her as the program head.

To Amy's credit, once she began to take an objective look at how her anger at her mother was driving some of her reactions, she courageously did the difficult work required to recover her professional momentum. Within a couple of months, Amy was able to put her reactions into perspective and apologize to Cindy. Within six months, Amy started behaving more consistently and considerately with everyone else—from her staff to her husband.

One of the most admirable qualities about Charmers is that if it takes changing behavior to keep moving forward, then this is precisely what the results-oriented Charmer will do. While the drive and ambition that takes them to the top can also be the source of their setbacks, when a Charmer decides to change something—look out! Change is coming. This also applies to the Charmer's ability to change themselves.

Conclusion

Some of the most compelling figures on the world stage are Charmers. Dazzled by the emotional intensity they are able to project, Pleasers and Commanders in particular may feel envious when the Charmer seems to bend the rules and jump to the head of the class. However, when we take the time to look beneath the image they project, we start to understand that Charmers aren't just rushing toward personal gain in the outer world. Frequently, they are also running away from painful feelings in their inner world.

When Charmers stop rushing around long enough to recognize the source of their ambition, they often become extraordinary change agents. A Charmer who has learned to use his or her sway and strategic insight for more than personal gain is a force to be reckoned with. Make no mistake about it: we need Charmers in our organizations, and we all need to learn to master the strengths of the Charmer if we want to get ahead.

CHAPTER FIVE

Charmer Power Plays

When Charmers describe what gets them excited, it tends to sound like a high-stakes game show. The focus is on who's winning, who's losing, and where the latest tally of cash and prizes stands. Few things are more engaging than working around a Charmer who's playing for high stakes. Whether it's a poker championship in Las Vegas or an investment banking deal on Wall Street, when a seasoned Charmer enters the fray, everyone plays the game at a higher level.

One of the Charmer's greatest gifts is the ability to shape other people's perceptions of reality—from peers and colleagues to their top managers. While other types on the grid may consider the Charmer's talent for "sculpting the facts" to be manipulative and dishonest, from the Charmer's perspective it's just common sense. However, what plagues Charmers most on the job is the feedback that is directed their way. Because we have noted that this feedback comes most frequently from peers, our work indicates that managing laterally presents a special challenge for the Charmer.

While they often have some trust issues to work through, the consistent virtue of people with Charmer power genes is their ability to produce top-notch results. They are strategic, thoughtful, and capable of incredible self-control when it comes to getting what they want. If they decide *what they want* is to improve their operating style with others, they often become dramatic success stories.

When the Charmer Is the Boss

While they are notoriously good rainmakers, Charmers hit their blind spots in managerial positions when they overlook the importance of building strong relationships with subordinates. In their haste to get ahead, Charmers may inadvertently lose the respect of their direct reports either by failing to acknowledge their expertise or by allowing suppressed frustration to seep out in public. Here are some rules of thumb for Charmer managers.

Make Sure Your Subordinates Feel Heard

Charmers must remember to make the time not only to listen to key staff members, but also to make sure these subordinates feel heard. Driven by their desire to advance, Charmers are often guilty of failing to acknowledge people who aren't senior enough to abruptly change their professional fate. Thus, some Charmers are only dimly aware of the existence of their subordinates until they need something from them. This puts Charmers at risk because they often don't get the feedback they need from key staff members until it's too late. As Charmers find the courage to slow down and face the buried feelings that are setting their hectic pace, they gradually learn to communicate more effectively with people at all levels of seniority. As this happens, Charmers not only become aware of the value of their subordinates, they often tend to blossom into valuable mentors.

Get Perspective on the Risks You Are Taking

Charmers have a talent for deflecting people's attention from unpleasant subjects. Unfortunately for them, Charmers also tend to be good at hiding things from themselves that they'd prefer not to know. Taking risks is one of the main areas where Charmers prefer to operate in the dark. When Charmers isolate themselves, they have a tendency to make plans, assess risks, and prioritize initiatives without consulting others. Depending on the scale of the organization they are working for, this type of detached working style can present a multitude of problems. First, the Charmer who doesn't run their ideas past key staff members may lose perspective on the magnitude and types of risks they are taking. What's more, by keeping their team out of the loop, Charmers don't always have a backup should a project go off the rails. When you share the risk, you also create a group that gets to share the credit. Charmers wise enough to keep others involved learn that sharing credit doesn't dilute their victory when they place their bets wisely. In fact, it magnifies everyone's enthusiasm.

Look for Opportunities to Express Sincere Appreciation

This is one of those "new habits" that Charmers need to cultivate through relentless repetition. Because many of them have been conditioned to discount others and look out for themselves, Charmers need to challenge themselves to notice the positive contributions of others. In the early stages of coaching, some Charmers find it helpful to establish a goal of finding two to three staff members a day who they can sincerely thank for the quality of their work. Much as one would go to the gym to exercise a flabby muscle, Charmers must learn to strengthen their capacity for expressing appreciation until it becomes an automatic reflex.

Focus on What's Best for the Group

Some of the other power types, Inspirers in particular, can only respect a boss who appears to be focused on what they can do for the group—not what the group can do for them. Developing this type of mind-set can be tricky for Charmers. This is because, in childhood, the Charmer's attention was virtually eclipsed by a needy parent. Admittedly, over time Charmers learned how to "work" (that is, manipulate) this parent, but that doesn't change the fact that the Charmer's earliest conditioning caused him or her to view the entire world through the lens of what was needed to keep this caregiver calm. Later in life, on the job, the Charmer often learns to frame challenges in terms of how it affects his or her influence over *one person at a time*. This is why we frequently hear feedback from frustrated subordinates who claim, "The last person in her office is the one she listens to!" To lead effectively, the Charmer must learn to appreciate how his or her behavior is affecting the group dynamic. This may require sacrificing some influence with selected people in the short term to do what's best for the group in the long term.

Power Grid Case Study: When Charmers Go It Alone

When Bonnie, a Charmer, was appointed to be the new head of fundraising for a nonprofit organization dedicated to helping women below the poverty line, she got a hard lesson in how important it is to listen to staff members.

One of the direct reports who Bonnie inherited along with the job was the office manager, Toni, who managed the books for this nonprofit. Toni, a woman of Native American descent, had been the lifeblood of the agency since its inception over a decade ago. Toni was an Inspirer.

Charmers often operate with a hidden agenda. For some, this agenda is so covert that they even manage to hide it from themselves. Bonnie grew up on the wrong side of the tracks in a small town where her brilliant mother never got the chance to pursue her own dreams of having a business and being on the town council. Every night, after Bonnie's physically exhausted father grunted a few words and fell into bed, her mother kept her up for hours chattering away about how Bonnie needed to remember how important it was to be noticed for her accomplishments in life. Over time, Bonnie internalized the need to live out her mother's unfulfilled dreams.

While she was throwing parties and networking like crazy to support struggling women, Bonnie's subliminal agenda was to land a column in a national women's magazine. In her mind's eye, Bonnie saw herself becoming a household name through her work with the poor. These daydreams were inspired by her lifelong ambition of having a career in politics. While she wasn't fully conscious of the connections in her own mind, Bonnie hazily dreamed of using the profile she could build running this nonprofit as a stepping-stone into politics. Driven by her childhood experiences, Bonnie was determined not to let anyone get in her way.

While Bonnie's internal motives were covert, her external actions were blatant. In her attempt to network her way to the top, Bonnie had been running through the nonprofit organization's modest budget at an alarming rate.

Bonnie got rather annoyed when Toni kept nagging her about expenses all the time. (Never forget how committed Charmers can be about deflecting attention from what they'd prefer not to face in their organizations and in themselves.) Bonnie was content to watch Toni's lips move while hitting the "mute" button in her mind because she assumed that once the donations started pouring in, everyone would be happy. Because of her own value system, it didn't occur to Bonnie that Toni's commitment to frugality might be based on principle as well as practicality.

While a Charmer boss may think subordinates can't sense their apathy, Inspirers have a keen sense for when they are being tuned out. What's worse, once an Inspirer becomes convinced that their boss isn't listening, they often start planning their exit. If and when the Inspirer actually leaves, the Charmer is often shocked by how strongly other people in the system react to the Inspirer's departure.

Bonnie was totally unprepared for the crisis that hit her when Toni actually left. With tears in her eyes, one of the office assistants handed Bonnie a small envelope tied with a turquoise ribbon. Inside was Toni's succinct and gracious resignation. Toni had headed back to her reservation in the mountains of Tennessee for the summer with her son. She was embarking on a vision quest with some of her tribal elders and would not be reachable by phone, Internet, or fax for the next month. Toni ended her note by wishing them all well.

As she scrambled to regroup, Bonnie hired a coach. Her powers of persuasion and survival skills were stretched to the limit as she fought to keep her job.

Bonnie was able to rethink her perspective on the organization's priorities by studying the power styles of both the Inspirer and the Charmer—thus getting more perspective on her own strengths and looming blind spots. She was forced to rein in her entertainment expenses immediately, and in the course of doing so, she found herself implementing many of Toni's cost-cutting suggestions.

Through studying the strengths of the Pleaser, Bonnie started working on establishing a sense of presence that made others feel safe enough to share frank feedback with her. Getting this feedback was one thing. Coming to terms with how people actually felt about the way she had been operating was another matter entirely. Perhaps the toughest part of the coaching process for Bonnie was that she was also forced to do some emergency soul-searching as she worked to save her job.

To keep some of the organization's top donors from jumping ship, Bonnie had to ask for help. This is particularly tough for Charmers, who, as we know, often prefer to go it alone. However, when Bonnie had a frank talk with the remaining staff about how and why she needed their support, they rallied. When some of the staff members made it clear to her that they were supporting the organization and that she was on probation with them, Bonnie shocked them by reply-ing humbly that she understood completely.

In the ensuing months, some important changes took place around Bonnie—and within her. On the outside, once Bonnie's team realized that she needed them, they began to trust her more. On the inside, Bonnie was no longer using the nonprofit as a stepping-stone to per-sonal fame. Having to rely on others to recover from a professional setback gave Bonnie a personal appreciation of the struggles that many of the impoverished women seeking work were facing when they came to the organization for help. As with many Charmers who apply their talents to higher causes, regaining her professional foothold allowed Bonnie to become a powerful change agent.

When the Charmer Is a Peer

When Charmers are dealing with their peers, they need to remain mind-ful of their tendency to come across as glib and slick on the outside when their competitive juices start flowing too freely on the inside. The outer battles the Charmer invents with key peers often echo the inner battle playing out between conflicting forces within their personali-ties. Because Charmers have been acclimated to secrecy and intrigue in their family systems, even simple job challenges can become dramatic when a Charmer enters the fray. The intensity that Charmers exude reflects the friction taking place between the contrasting layers of their personalities. This intensity makes it impossible to ignore Charmers. It also makes it difficult for their peers to relax around them. I'll men-tion a few things Charmers should keep in mind to win the hearts and minds of their peers.

Pick Your Battles Carefully

Charmers, particularly those whose ambition is fueled by the need to distract themselves from uncomfortable feelings, can find a myriad of formal and informal ways to compete with their peers. Because they often needed to manipulate their parents to survive emotionally, for some Charmers a nonstop undercurrent of gamesmanship is seething beneath the surface of their professional relationships. This undercurrent of tension can become particularly acute when the Charmer feels that a colleague may be besting them in some way. One clue that a Charmer is feeling threatened is that you can almost set your watch by the consistency of the explosions Charmers will have with a colleague they want to outshine. Until they have explored the reasons they feel compelled to constantly compare themselves with others, Charmers can be fatally attracted to one-upping their most valuable peers. That said, once a Charmer is able to break free from the habit of needing to best others in subtle ways, the energy for constructive change that is released can be formidable. Because the Charmer is no longer distracted by petty dramas, their strategic potential is freed up to focus on the big picture. Charmers who have reconditioned themselves to pick their battles wisely make powerful business alliances and tend to rise to the top of their organizations.

Don't Underestimate Your Colleagues

Underestimating a peer can be a dangerous career move for a Charmer. Because they were falsely empowered by a needy parent, Charmers are often lulled into believing that they are superior to their colleagues. Nobody is saying the Charmer isn't smart. However, as one frustrated peer put it to a Charmer in a management meeting, "Nobody's claiming that you aren't the smartest person in the room. What we are *are* saying is that the rest of us aren't as dumb as you think we are." Charmers must remember that they don't have the leverage in the workplace to emotionally manipulate their peers that they may have had with a needy parent. Thus, Charmers managing laterally need to keep their egos in check.

Be Prepared for Direct Confrontation

Since Charmers often grew up accustomed to covert guerrilla warfare, they may be caught off guard by the more direct power plays other power types invoke to protect their turf or establish their superiority. This is a particularly important point when the Charmer's peer is a Commander. Both the Charmer and the Commander rely heavily on their respective images to move up in the workplace. However, the image the Charmer projects often rests largely on personal mystique, while the image of the Commander has often been more patiently established to ensure that the full force of the system rests behind it. When the Charmer encounters a Commander, it can be a golden opportunity to learn to operate more powerfully on the job. Going head-to-head with a Commander often involves fighting a fair fight in the clear light of day. By practicing the art of direct confrontation, Charmers can learn to believe in their cause and in themselves at a deeper level.

Know When to Turn the Charm Off

To establish trust with peers who are interacting with them on a regular basis, Charmers sometimes have to drop the act and just get real. This can be a challenge for Charmers who feel compelled to manage others' perceptions of them as carefully as possible. Because of their tendency to be self-protective on the job, Charmers often believe that strategy is far more important than social interaction with their peers. As a result, when a colleague tries to take a minute to "chat" with a Charmer, the Charmer's mind often explodes with a laundry list of more pressing matters. However, it's in precisely these less structured moments that the Charmer may get the opportunity to build the professional alliances necessary to see some of their more ambitious plans through to completion.

Power Grid Case Study:
A Charmer Learns to Collaborate

Pete (a Charmer) and Ted (a Commander) are both aspiring foreign exchange traders who've gotten their first shot at management during their firm's recent reorganization. Unfortunately, since they've been thrust together as coheads, the opportunity is a challenge for them on multiple levels. These two had never been fond of each other, but because they both maintained an upbeat "game face" for senior management, their superiors had no idea of the can of worms that had been opened by thrusting these men into a forced collaboration.

Pete had been isolating himself for most of his life. The only child from a privileged family, Pete grew up in the eye of a social hurricane. Both of Pete's parents came from old money, and both of them got bored easily—especially with each other. His mother and father both had a steady stream of extramarital affairs, and, while they never formally divorced, they began to live separately while Pete was still in grammar school.

By his early teens, Pete was so weary of feeling like a pawn in his parents' never-ending romantic games that he began to retreat into books and puzzles to find some peace. In school, Pete was considered a math prodigy. He effortlessly made top marks, and in spite of the fact that he had little patience for networking and interviewing, his academic honors won him several top job offers upon graduation.

As the most profitable trader on the desk, Pete was furious about the cohead arrangement because he felt that the job was rightfully his. Here's where Pete lost perspective. First, many people in the department hated his arrogance. Pete didn't know this, of course, because, like many Charmers, he didn't get the feedback he needed to be objective about how others experienced his behavior. Second, one of the secrets of Pete's profitability was that he occasionally operated outside his trading limits. Pete didn't think anyone knew about this.

Ted knew.

Ted had been getting an earful for years from demoralized traders who were sick of Pete's constant reminders that he was the best trader on the desk. What was even more dangerous, Ted also knew that Pete didn't have any kind of consistent model for his trading style. Pete operated by the seat of his pants. In the current risk environment, senior management would be terrified if they realized this. What's more, like many Charmers, Pete had become so conditioned to seek advantage any way he could that he had been hiding the magnitude of the risks he was taking, even from himself.

Pete got really nervous when he realized that Ted, with the support of senior management, was working on a departmental overview of all their risk management systems. Pete had no "system." What he had were great gut instincts and warm personal chats with their bosses that, together, kept people from sticking their noses into how he was producing those stellar returns.

To save his career, and the firm's reputation, Pete was going to have to build a better rapport with Ted. Since Ted was a Commander, this was going to take more than a warm smile and a pat on the back at the local pub. Pete, who had gotten away with operating as a lone wolf for most of his career, reached out for coaching to get the tools he needed to collaborate with Ted.

Pete started studying the power style of the Commander so he could deal more directly with Ted. He swallowed his pride and set up a series of meetings with Ted to face the inevitable. In the process of conferring openly with Ted on how they could work together to create a more reliable risk management system, Pete made an important discovery. As he changed his behavior and began to treat Ted with more respect on the outside, his inner attitude toward Ted began to improve as well.

Much to his surprise, Pete found that he actually enjoyed studying the power style of the Commander. Looking at the situation through the lens of what was best for the firm, rather than what was best for his own pocketbook, gave Pete a new perspective on an old challenge. Pete, who had always loved puzzles, quickly came to the conclusion that creating a new risk management system was much more exciting than gaming the old one that he had been outsmarting for years.

Pete and Ted both gradually developed a grudging respect for one another. As they learned to trust each other's judgment, they also came to the mutual conclusion that it was easier to cohead than it might have been for either of them to run the department alone.

When the Charmer Is a Subordinate

Charmers have learned to equate emotional survival with staying in control of the people who are supposed to be in control of them. Since Charmers are often fearful that any person or group with authority over them will drain their emotional energy the way a needy parent did in their childhood, they consider staying in control to be a matter of self-preservation. As they cultivate the balance necessary to give to others without losing themselves, Charmers become less defensive around authority figures.

Don't Make Promises You Can't Keep

Charmers need to establish realistic expectations in terms of what they are accountable for that they can stick to long term. This is particularly important when the Charmer is getting to know a new boss. Since they learned how to play up to authority figures early in life, they often go through a honeymoon period with a new superior. During the initial phase of this new relationship, Charmers lavish the boss with attention and try to learn everything they can. What Charmers are often trying to learn is how to put together a strategy that will eventually enable them to get the most credit for the least amount of work. Unfortunately, as the boss gets seduced by all this attention, they may assume that the Charmer will always be at their beck and call. If the Charmer doesn't stick to their day job, they may risk getting burned out.

Come Clean When You Make a Mistake

Rules are merely suggestions for the Charmer who secretly thinks he or she is smarter than the rule makers. If their caregivers were ineffective disciplinarians, the Charmer may have been set up to fail later in life. One of the primary ways they fail is by underestimating the people around them and trying to deflect blame rather than facing the consequences when they are at fault. The longer this goes on, and the subtler it is, the harder it can be on the Charmer's career momentum. Charmers shouldn't assume that just because their boss doesn't say anything about a matter they have tried to sweep under the rug, the problem hasn't been noticed. In many cases, Charmers discover that their superiors have been keeping a careful tally of their unacknowledged errors. It's best for Charmers to learn to come clean with managers when they've made a significant mistake, and address how they'll solve the problem at hand.

Be Prepared for Concrete Consequences

Once Charmers have left the overly forgiving arms of a needy caregiver, they must accept that they will face concrete consequences for performance slips. This is particularly true in the workplace. When Charmers end up reporting to a boss who expects them to respect authority and play by the rules, those who grew up without being held accountable are sometimes caught off guard. Professional accountability sets the bar way above the comfort zone of those Charmers who learned in childhood to manipulate authority figures and bend the rules to suit themselves. Suddenly, when they don't play by the rules, Charmers find that they are being passed over for promotion, left off key projects, and even getting their pay docked. The good news here is that when they accept that it's in their best interest to comply, Charmers are remarkably quick learners and will fall into line accordingly.

What's more, when experiencing discipline increases their respect for their boss, Charmers will often start to outperform to get the relationship with their superior back on track.

Learn to Listen to Those with Authentic Power

Charmers are often surprised to realize that a boss who forces them to stop cutting corners and calls them on the carpet when they are not doing their best work can have a positive and powerful ability to motivate them. The secret to this is simple. Although Charmers were falsely empowered by a needy parent, like all of us they long to be part of something greater than themselves. We all want to believe in something or someone. Charmers had difficulty believing in their caregivers because their caregivers often didn't believe in themselves. Authentic leaders can come from any quadrant on the Power Grid, and we believe in them because they hold themselves accountable, they hold us accountable, and they hold on to the vision the organization is focused on achieving. Once they learn to listen to an authentic leader, even the evasive Charmer begins to feel the stirrings of something noble being activated within them.

Power Grid Case Study: A Charmer Learns to Calibrate Expectations

We'll return to the story of Dave, a Charmer who is the general manager of a restaurant and resort, and his boss, Bryan, a Pleaser. By revisiting the story, this time from the Charmer's perspective, you'll see how people with opposing power styles can interpret the same situation quite differently.

Bryan inherited his family's business and is counting on Dave to make the tough business decisions and keep the staff in line. As is frequently the case when the Charmer is a subordinate, the beginning of Dave and Bryan's working relationship felt like a whirlwind courtship. Dave sparkled in the interview process, and nothing seemed like too much for him during his first six months on the job. He reviewed the budget, rearranged the responsibilities of key staff members, and even revamped the resort's advertising campaign. In the course of these achievements, he managed to convince his boss and the rest of the staff that the place couldn't run without him.

Dave, who basically felt he had landed a dream job, was surprised when, after the first six months, he realized that Bryan's calls and meeting requests were starting to irritate him. After all, Dave was working for a Pleaser who basically let him run things his own way as long as they had some brainstorming sessions. Charmers, who are often loners at heart, long for a job where they can operate as autonomously as possible. Logically, Dave felt that the personal chats Bryan craved should have been a small price to pay for the independence he was being given, but like many Charmers who begin to isolate themselves on the job, Dave didn't understand the emotions that were driving him.

Unfortunately, Bryan, like many Pleasers, was a man who felt entitled to share his emotional problems along with his professional visions once he felt he had "connected" with a colleague. Pleasers often assume that sharing personal feelings brings people closer. However, Charmers struggle with a self-protective instinct that can border on a phobia when it comes to their fear of being emotionally engulfed by a needy authority figure.

Suddenly, Dave couldn't bear to get out of bed on Monday morning to face another minute of Bryan's yammering about his problems with his wife, his problems with the staff, or his personal take on anything. Dave began coming into work late, sneaking around to avoid Bryan, and doing everything he could to not have to deal with his boss.

While Charmers don't trust easily, they often have an inner circle of family and close friends in their lives who they rely on consistently. One person who helped Dave through this tough spot was his best friend from college, John. When John came by Dave's house to pick him up for dinner one night, he found Dave holed up in his home office, considering new job opportunities. "What's the problem, Dave?" John asked with obvious concern. "I thought you loved this job." When Dave was able to articulate his concerns to his friend, John pointed out a connection that saved Dave's job and potentially his career. "Of course Bryan is getting to you," John told him thoughtfully. "He's acting just like your mother." Dave's mother, who was an emotionally needy drinker, used to drain Dave with her endless demands for emotional support. The helplessness Dave felt as a child caused him to operate at the fear-based extreme of the y-axis. By identifying this connection, John made it possible for Dave to set the professional boundaries he needed to continue to function in a job he loved.

The self-identified Charmers I've worked with have frequently told me that reading about the power style of Pleasers has helped them understand why it's so critical to set up realistic expectations with their boss. While personal chats with the boss may help the Charmer land a job or secure a promotion, such a practice also establishes a standard of availability that the Charmer may come to resent down the line. To maximize their power and not flame out, Charmers need to train their boss (and themselves) to set sustainable norms for the long term.

Conclusion

Charmers who take the time to do sincere soul-searching can blossom into captivating change agents. Our clients who analyze the biographies of leaders such as John F. Kennedy, Maya Angelou, and Henry Ford are surprised to learn how many people who have changed the face of our world grew up in what could be characterized as a Charmer family system.

The trick to working with Charmers is getting past their defenses so you can persuade them to focus their talents on the greater good. Whether you suspect you might be a Charmer or you might be working with one, it's important to remember that the door to self-examination opens from the inside. As far as the Charmer and personal growth are concerned, you can't rush them, you can't bribe them, and it's pretty hard to scare them. That said, when they finally make the decision to look within, you can't stop them. When a Charmer is ready to grow, they tend to become powerful forces for good, and they usually bring the rest of us right along with them.

CHAPTER SIX

Meet the Commander

If Commanders had a common mantra, it would be "Results now!" Whether they are taking a hill in a military siege or taking control in a boardroom, the power of a Commander stems from their ability to exude a decisive confidence and a drive to win that foster a sense of urgency in others. When participants in our workshops are asked to identify people they think exemplify the four power styles, Jack Welch is one of the most frequently cited when it comes to the power style of the Commander. Other people who are regularly mentioned include Norman Schwarzkopf, Margaret Thatcher, and George Washington.

A Commander's power genes tend to propel them all the way to the highest levels of formal power. Thus, while 15 percent of the clients from *Fortune* 500 companies we have worked with consider themselves Commanders, it is noteworthy that over 80 percent of this subset who self-identify with the Commander power style are either CEOs or executives operating at the highest levels of seniority.

Strengths of the Commander

Commanders stand apart because not only are they comfortable in positions of leadership, they also offer unwavering support of the leaders above them in an organization. They are decisive, resilient, and adaptable.

A Strong Will to Win

Ready for battle at a moment's notice, Commanders face many aspects of life—personal life, work life, and family life—with an action-oriented focus on their advancement.

Whether they are participants or loyal fans, many Commanders love sports and use tips from the playing field to help them squarely face their professional battles. For example, Jack Welch kicks off his autobiography, *Jack: Straight from the Gut,* by discussing the life lessons he drew from playing hockey in high school.[1] Once the starting gun goes off on the first day of their first job, not only will Commanders do whatever it takes to get ahead, because of their innate understanding of how things work in a hierarchy, but they also keep their eye on the prize. The prize, as Commanders define it, is upward mobility within their organizations.

Respect for Authority

The way Commanders define success ensures that these men and women will strive to please their bosses. While this drive to manage up may make them look like yes-men at times, it's important to remember that this mentality also makes them strong team players who are committed to maintaining the power structure of which they are a part. Because of this, Commanders operate at the formal end of the x-axis on the Power Grid, valuing order and tying advancement and compensation tightly to merit and loyalty.

When it comes to identifying with the system in which they operate,

Commanders not only drink the Kool-Aid—they go back for a second cup. Rather than questioning authority, they support it, because they are set on trying to achieve that authority themselves. Keenly sensitive of how informal power within a group can eventually transform into formal authority over it, Commanders routinely evaluate how their reactions are influencing their place in the pecking order of any system. They derive power from that system, drawing from the group's energy as a whole.

Since they crave status, Commanders seek environments in which a particular hierarchical system confers prestige. Commanders are known for attending the "right" schools, taking the "right" courses, and marrying the "right" people to support their ambitions early in the game. After college, they tend to work for companies that represent a compelling corporate brand. Most of the Commanders we have coached selected colleges based on the quality of their sports programs, their science and technology faculty, or their alumni network.

After graduation, Commanders are often drawn to powerful, large companies where they can flex their high-performance muscles. The bigger the hierarchy, the more power they get to command once they reach the top. This is one reason why, at the beginning of their careers, Commanders are often more attracted to junior positions in large organizations than they are to midlevel positions in start-ups. Thus, a company's brand is critical when it comes to recruiting Commanders.

Because they derive much of their sense of identity from being part of a successful system, the Commander's entrepreneurial instincts often don't kick in until later in their careers. For example, I've worked with many talented Commanders who started successful investment boutiques *after* rising through the ranks in large investment institutions. However, this type of second-stage entrepreneurship that occurs in mature industries differs from the entrepreneurial journey that typically characterizes Inspirers. Inspirers are more likely to have one of those "Wright Brothers moments" that occur when they are off fishing or walking in the woods and the idea for a new invention strikes them.

No-Nonsense, Decisive Leaders

Valuing winning above enjoying the game means that Commanders are frequently able to compartmentalize their feelings, eschewing emotion from business decisions. They are often seen as no-nonsense, decisive leaders; when it comes to making tough calls during difficult times, nobody gets down to business like a Commander. Commanders can be so unsentimental about executing tough business decisions that they can toast your family at an office Christmas party and fire you early the next morning without missing a beat. (It is noteworthy that a Commander I coached who actually did this was filled with private remorse over this situation. However, because he felt it was his duty to keep up his "game face" for the firm, the behavior he exhibited with his colleagues was inscrutable.)

While it may be a bit chilling for their employees, the Commander's ability to compartmentalize their feelings and stay focused on the bottom line has its obvious professional rewards. For example, the Commander's insistence on putting the appropriate processes and procedures in place can be a saving grace in organizations. You're not going to find a Commander rewarding employees for sentimental reasons. A strong Commander will save a firm a great deal of money. In many cases, they can save their firms from lawsuits as well. Commanders also tend to take responsibility for their decisions. They will take the heat to be accountable for a tough call.

Resilience

A martial arts instructor once told me that the secret to winning a fight was being the one who could keep getting up after taking a hit— Commanders exemplify this strength. In the business world, Commanders are often able to summon the courage and endurance necessary to succeed in new business ventures that can create widespread economic opportunities for their organizations. They are resilient and determined, and are prepared to withstand a great deal of pressure on the battlefield to get ahead—often more than others realize.

When the going gets tough, Commanders keep going. They will take a bullet for the boss, work late for the boss, and even put up with incredible mood swings from the boss if that's what it takes to advance. Situations that cause other power types to recoil or resign often don't even faze a hard-core Commander.

Adaptability

Commanders don't quit, they just morph. As noted above, Commanders who are able to take control of their power reflexes, rather than being controlled by them, often develop the agility they need to integrate the strengths from other quadrants to enhance their natural leadership qualities. Jack Welch is a prime example of this. In his current role, in partnership with his wife, Suzy, Jack has established himself as an educator, leadership expert, and dedicated husband. This new alignment has enabled him to continue to support professional systems while achieving the personal balance that eludes many hard-charging Commanders who, like Welch, end up grappling with divorce in the earlier stages of their ascent. The power style that propelled Welch's famous rise at General Electric was that of a classic Commander. His new professional platform showcases Welch's ability to refine his power reflexes so that he exhibits a combination of the strengths we associate with both the Commander and the Inspirer.

Self-Confidence

Hand in hand with their will to win—and their ability to keep trying—Commanders' natural confidence elicits the admiration of those around them. It is also a key ingredient to their recipe for gaining power. This aura only gets stronger as the Commander gets more authentic. No matter how much people criticize them, gossip about them, or gripe about them, most people secretly admire Commanders and fantasize about gaining their ability to elicit respect. I've often had the privilege of working with Commanders whose teams have sworn loyalty to them through thick and thin because they know this leader will come out on top if it's humanly possible.

The Commander's Blind Spots

While the Commander may have an easier time than most at exerting their authority, they too have blind spots that hinder more fruitful relationships with their bosses, peers, and subordinates. Their determination to win is often accompanied by a deep-seated fear of losing control. A nuance worth noting here is that while Charmers also want to get ahead and stay in control, Charmers are often willing to concede small victories to the people around them while they plot privately to win the points that have the most strategic value to them in the long term. In contrast, when Commanders are dancing with their dark side, losing control even for a minute can feel tantamount to losing the game.

The danger for a Commander grappling with his or her blind spots is that the distinction between the latest battle and the overall war can get fuzzy. When they are operating on automatic pilot, Commanders may believe that coming in second on anything is not an option—it can feel like a matter of principle to them. This type of all-or-nothing thinking causes Commanders to fall back on power reflexes that may be effective in some cases but, in the long term, can end up hurting their colleagues, their businesses, and their careers.

Valuing the System over the Individual

A natural extension of the Commander's commitment to getting a top spot in their system is their enthusiasm for protecting the system itself. For a Commander, the "greater good" is always aligned with supporting the system that supports them. Because of this, Commanders on autopilot are often so focused on following the rules that they may inadvertently act as if the rules are more important than the people the rules are designed to support.

Many Commanders resonate with the way the military keeps people focused on serving the system. In his autobiography, *It Doesn't Take a Hero,* four-star general Norman Schwarzkopf gives us a glimpse into the way that symbols of prestige can be a powerful incentive for Commanders when he writes, "The Army, with its emphasis on ranks and medals and efficiency reports, is the easiest institution in the world in which to get consumed with ambition. Some officers spend all their time currying favor and worrying about their next promotion."[2]

When their blind spots kick in, Commanders may be unaware of when their individual judgment has been eclipsed by groupthink. When enough of them get clustered at the top of a system, and they often do because they work well in packs, the system itself may lose the capacity to recognize potential problems and reinvent itself in changing times. Thus, the Commanders holding the most powerful positions within their systems can sometimes be the most passive about changing these systems.

Thus, the Commanders' admirable qualities of loyalty and respect for authority can start to work against them if they tend to base their decisions exclusively on the views of colleagues at their own rank or above.

Intolerance and Insensitivity

Commanders can come across as gruff and demanding, using a tone that intimidates those who dare to cross them—and even those who don't. Whether on behalf of themselves or their professions, Commanders' ability to compartmentalize business and emotion often means that business wins the upper hand. Thus, in many cases, the emotional impact of their words on others isn't considered. Commanders grappling with this blind spot fail to communicate with patience and tact. Jack Welch learned the costs of his harsh interpersonal style early in his career when he was almost kept off the list of CEO prospects by GE's head of human resources in the 1970s, Roy Johnson. Welch found out that Johnson was concerned that he intimidated his subordinates and drove too hard for results.

Impatience

One line that makes many of my CEO clients laugh is, "If something takes any time at all, it takes too long for a Commander." Work and life are a series of battles to be won for the Commander, and they are usually looking past the meeting they are in or the conversation they are having right now to the future challenges they must overcome. Whatever the matter is at hand, the Commander will impatiently expect the issue to be resolved according to their rules, yesterday, and with minimal input from them.

Because of their tendency to be impatient, Commanders have a myriad of nonverbal cues they exude that telegraph, "Get to the point fast!" While there are times that this is a valuable skill, there are times when it's equally valuable to be able to put others (particularly subordinates) at ease. In the course of coaching, I've been given feedback from numerous people reporting to Commanders that shows how quickly employees shut down and fail to communicate vital information when the body language, facial expression, or vocal tone of their superior conveys impatience. Comments such as "He gets testy, folds his arms, and furrows his brow when members of the executive committee want to brainstorm . . . It's not worth the career risk to irritate him by exploring the deeper implications of the challenges we are facing" convey how costly this blind spot can be to organizations, shareholders, and ultimately the professional reputations of the Commanders themselves.

Commanders struggling with a blind spot around impatience can also get a little touchy when asked to explain the rationale behind their initiatives. After all, the Commander is used to giving commands, not explanations. As a result, Commanders can be vulnerable when the need arises to communicate persuasively with people operating from other quadrants on the grid.

In the early stages of learning to use the Power Grid, some Commanders I have worked with have confessed to feeling that even simple requests to explain their position seem insubordinate. In short order, these Commanders learn that the career risk of their reluctance to communicate thoughtfully with others is that colleagues throughout their organizations may incorrectly assume that they are either uncaring or uninformed.

Tunnel Vision

As with Charmers, the emotional reflexes of the Commander are driven by their anxious drive to always come out on top. However, while Charmers are driven to succeed on their own terms, Commanders are often conditioned to let authority figures and their organizations define success for them. Thus, Commanders often struggle with tunnel vision. Commanders who rarely allow their decisions to be questioned can easily lose perspective on a problem.

Having been conditioned to stay focused on making top grades, being a star athlete, or networking with the "right people," many Commanders have been so busy rushing to achieve the goals set for them by others that they have had little time to reflect on why they are pursuing these goals in the first place. (Note that while Pleasers acquiesce in this way in order to receive approval, Commanders are simply following the plans and procedures dictated by their authority figures.) In their haste to get ahead, both Commanders and Charmers tend to avoid self-reflection. However, while the Charmer is often running away from inner demons, the Commander is often rushing to achieve external recognition within their organization. Thus, Commanders tend to let their organizations create the playing field, define the scoring system, and evaluate their performance. They tend to be in such a hurry to advance according to the rules others have created that they rarely question the rules themselves at a deeper level.

As we shall see when we examine their family systems, many Commanders are only dimly aware that when it comes to doing something like picking a college or a major course of study, they have usually had someone else doing their thinking for them for years. Even when their early path in life is smoothed by a parent who ensures admission to their alma mater, Commanders can feel boxed in by this type of sheltering prestige. To gain true control over their lives and their careers, Commanders need to recognize their own agency in making choices about what they want—and they need to look beyond the boxes defined for them by others to assess the full range of alternatives and opportunities.

Because so many Commanders achieve senior management positions, it is important to note that tunnel vision can manifest itself as insularity at the senior executive level. Battle-weary Commanders who don't want to summon the energy it takes to process controversial feedback may inadvertently surround themselves with people who tell them what they want to hear. This is a blind spot that needs to be addressed if the Commander wants to be a leader who's able to deal with uncomfortable truths and adapt to changing circumstances.

A Commander's Family Background

The Commander's family structure is typically a hierarchy—and what the dominant figures in that structure demanded of the Commander as a child. Most Commanders have one parent who is a Commander themselves. One lesson that Commander parents frequently impart is, "If you don't play to win, don't bother to play."

Commanders typically grow up in a family system that models rigid adherence to order, rules, and hierarchies. Many Commanders come from highly disciplined military families or families that are extraordinarily devoted to religious or political causes. In a Commander's family system, everything depends on an individual's position in the hierarchy.

In this rigid hierarchical structure, often one parent is firmly in charge. The other parent, along with the children, ends up vying for the approval and support of the parent running the show. For example, in Jack Welch's family, while Welch's father, John, was a railroad conductor and the primary breadwinner, his mother, Grace, headed the household and was the disciplinarian of the family. Welch notes that if he got in trouble, his father would tell his mother, who would then confront him and dole out what she deemed to be the appropriate punishment. Welch writes, "If I have any leadership style, any way of getting the best out of people, I owe it to her."[3] In his autobiography, he cites her compassion and generosity, but also her tendency to hold a grudge—and the similarities between them.

One of the side effects of a family system where power is not shared equally between both parents, but is predominantly centered in one of them, is that all members of this system must adjust to an ongoing imbalance between giving and taking. All members of this system internalize the unspoken rules that govern their "place" in the family hierarchy. If one of the children or the disempowered parent has a helpful idea, it's irrelevant unless the parent in power agrees. In this type of system, it's all about rank.

Dan's early experience in his family system illustrates this dynamic. Dan's father, Rick, was a defense contractor who ruled his family with an iron fist.

Dan's dream was to attend art school and become a comic book illustrator. His father felt he should focus on a more sensible business career so that he would be able to support a family. One night, Dan and his father argued over his dreams for his future so vehemently that Dan stormed away from the dinner table and ended up sulking on the front porch. His mother, Rachel, tiptoed out between courses to check on her son. Dan looked up at her and cried out in frustration, "It's my life! You know he's being selfish to try and make me do what he wants. Times have changed—I can make it as an artist!"

After a moment of silence, Rachel quietly reminded her son, "It doesn't matter if he's wrong; he's still your father." This family's rigid hierarchy left only one individual as the decision maker.

Not surprisingly, Dan bowed to his father's wishes and ended up pursuing a degree in business administration. He then went on to become a financial analyst. A Commander who was used to having a system to support him, Dan was adrift for months professionally when his firm downsized and he was between jobs. In fact, when he realized he was going to have to "sell himself," Dan spent his first couple of transitional months hiding in his basement, surfing the Net to avoid people. However, once he learned how to work with the Power Grid, Dan began to appreciate the value of cultivating some of the interpersonal strengths more commonly associated with Pleasers and Charmers. As he began to practice listening more thoughtfully to others, Dan also started listening more thoughtfully to himself. When he did return to the workforce, he joined an Internet marketing company that incorporated graphic design as part of the strategy used to help clients reach customers around the world. This company's focus tapped into Dan's lifelong passion for the visual arts.

The types of hierarchical family systems that condition people to become Commanders are often strictly focused on early achievement and high performance. Everything is about winning. Jack Welch, for example, opens his autobiography with the foundational story of his mother storming into the locker room after he had thrown his hockey stick in frustration at the end of a losing game. "Every eye was glued on this middle-aged woman in a floral patterned dress . . . [s]he went right for me, grabbing the top of my uniform. 'You punk!' she shouted in my face. 'If you don't know how to lose, you'll never know how to win. If you don't know this, you shouldn't be playing.'"[4] Even losing right was a part of winning, as Welch's domineering mother makes clear in no uncertain terms.

This kind of constant drive to achieve has a number of potentially negative ramifications. Many educational specialists believe that when a child is pushed too hard, the child may become overly competitive.[5] Kids who become overly competitive often begin to believe that winning is more important than how they play the game. As a result, they may cut corners and even cheat to come out on top. When this behavior takes place on the dodgeball field, it's a problem for their parents and their teachers; when it takes place on Capitol Hill or on Wall Street, it's a problem for us all. These may be drastic examples, but the Commander's struggle to mount the hierarchy they were exposed to in childhood can have a serious impact, as we have seen with Jack Welch and how he intimidated his subordinates.

Children from systems so focused on achievement are rarely allowed unstructured time to let their imaginations wander. While forgetting to exercise the imagination may seem like an innocent oversight in a competitive world, an overly structured childhood comes with some costs.

The damaging side effect of depriving kids of the time to daydream is that while their muscles may be toned from varsity sports, their imaginations are getting flabby. Without a fine-tuned imagination, you can't envision the world other than as it is today. When Commanders get so focused on outer achievement that they ignore their inner worlds, their imaginations get rusty. Bottom line: when our leaders can't imagine the world other than as it is today, they can't innovate—they can only replicate.

The Commander in Transition

Because they are so passionate about advancing within systems, Commanders often focus on their job as the basis for their identity. As a result, job transition is particularly difficult for the Commander. While most of us have financial anxiety and some professional insecurities in the wake of a corporate downsizing, Commanders are often particularly hard hit. Individuals from other quadrants can recharge with a little time off—a Pleaser might spend more time with their kids, Charmers may splurge on a lavish vacation, and Inspirers might start focusing on their next creative vision. Commanders, however, are plagued by insecurity in the face of an unexpected block of personal time. They find themselves frantically going through their Rolodex and looking for job interviews to get into a system that will reinforce their established sense of identity.

Job hunters frequently recite the adage "It's not what you know, but who you know." What this well-worn phrase forces the Commander to face is that he or she must be able to listen thoughtfully and communicate persuasively in one-on-one situations in order to interview effectively. Thus, it's often an unexpected job transition that encourages the Commander to cultivate the behavioral reflexes normally associated with Pleasers and Charmers as they network to try to find a new organization that will embrace their talents. Mastering the skills necessary to set a more effective personal tone with others not only makes Commanders more effective on the job, it also tends to enhance their personal self-esteem and overall life satisfaction.

As they transition into a new professional culture, it's important for Commanders to realize that the power they wield by leveraging the energy of a new group, while formidable, doesn't cure everything if the organization they join doesn't support their authentic talents and welcome their honest opinions.

A Commander in Action

Steve, the CEO of an asset management firm, is a Commander who has been groomed since birth to assume authority. Even as a child, Steve spoke to those around him in a commanding tone, which he learned by imitating his father, a self-made man who had transitioned from a distinguished career in military service to running his own commercial construction company.

When he joined the workforce and rose through the ranks in his industry, everything Steve did was designed to advance and protect his status. While many employees who reported to Steve resigned, citing Steve's short temper and cutting tone, he never reflected deeply about how his authoritarian style was affecting the people around him. When pressed, Steve would confess that he considered pondering the emotional dimension of business relationships to be a sentimental waste of time encouraged by people who didn't get the commercial point.

In spite of his gruff demeanor, Steve's focus on pleasing those he reported to and his ability to deliver results put his career in asset management on the fast track. A top performer both on the golf course and in the boardroom, Steve managed to achieve one promotion after the next as he steadily climbed the corporate ladder. While he had a reputation for having a quick temper, Steve was also known for being fair, decisive, and a tireless worker.

As his career progressed, Steve became so single-mindedly focused on projecting the "right" senior executive image to those above him that he began to systematically overlook the human dimension of keeping his organization functioning collaboratively. Steve was in such a rush to get ahead that he developed the bad habit of impatiently brushing off subordinates who told him things he didn't want to hear. Sadly for Steve, one of the long-term consequences of this habit was that employees will often hide controversial information from superiors who don't make them feel at ease.

Over the years, various people throughout the firm had tried to warn Steve that there were problems with the organization's IT systems and the financial reports they supported. Unfortunately for Steve, what had started as occasional impatience had developed into the self-destructive habit of "shooting the messenger" when he didn't like what he heard. Quite logically, most of Steve's direct reports got the hint and stopped trying to delve into these hot-button topics with him.

After he became CEO, Steve got an irate call from one of his firm's largest clients complaining about difficulty getting detailed information about a portfolio Steve's firm was running for them. When the client threatened to pull this crucial account if Steve's firm didn't get them the data they wanted quickly, Steve was caught completely off guard.

When the situation came to a head, with this important client on the verge of leaving, the board of directors began to consider replacing Steve. To get his firm and his job back on track, Steve needed to cultivate the capacity to look within. The first thing Steve had to do was get honest with himself. He had to come to terms with the ways his tunnel vision of his CEO image had caused him to ignore the mounting unrest that was brewing throughout his firm.

Once Steve had identified himself as a Commander, he realized that he had some powerful strengths to draw from. He knew that he was both adaptable and resilient. Through reflecting on the ways that his father had modeled the Commander's power style, Steve realized innately that no matter how hard it gets, Commanders have a way of reaching down inside themselves and drawing on reserves of courage and determination that can be nothing short of amazing to onlookers. As he became more conscious of ways he could draw on these strengths under pressure, Steve realized that he was selling himself short by thinking that it was only his title and its attendant prestige that commanded respect. As his perspective broadened, Steve was able to start developing a less insular approach to running his organization.

One of the first areas where Steve needed to make some changes was his approach to communicating with people at different levels of seniority. Overhauling his communication style forced Steve to study and attempt to cultivate some of the collaborative strengths that are frequently associated with Pleasers and Inspirers on the Power Grid. Working through his blind spots also required him to listen to people outside his inner circle and deal with the tough feedback he needed to hear to get his organization back on track. Like many Commanders struggling with tunnel vision, Steve had been limiting himself to the perspective of the top layer of management.

Studying the power styles of the Pleaser and the Inspirer also helped

Steve brush up on his listening skills. Morale in his firm skyrocketed as Steve proved to employees throughout the organization that he was willing to hear their opinions without punishing them. Over the ensuing months, Steve managed to save one of his firm's most important clients, hire a competent systems expert to run his IT division, dismantle his inner circle, and keep his job.

Conclusion

When you look around our world, you will note that many of the most respected leaders we rely on are Commanders. Their earliest life experiences have conditioned them to be decisive, reliable, and focused on winning the game. Reviewing the Commander power style teaches us that a great deal from this quadrant is worth emulating.

However, as we'll discuss in the next chapter, there's a downside to the conditioning that forges these dedicated business warriors. They often have their eyes so firmly fixed on the next rung in the ladder that they forget to look down, or even to look around, when it matters most.

CHAPTER SEVEN

Commander Power Plays

Who doesn't admire a Commander's passion for winning? Whether it's the stirring performance of George C. Scott portraying Patton, the legacy of Winston Churchill, or the celebrated coaches of the National Football League, we all find ourselves on the edge of our seats rooting for great heroic Commanders to seize the day.

When we consider how the power genes of the Commander play out in the workplace, it's important to note that over 65 percent of our clients who self-identify with this power style report that managing down is one of their biggest challenges. When I have solicited candid feedback about the Commanders I have coached, their colleagues often report that the Commander's project management skills consistently outshine his or her relational skills. This type of feedback may catch the Commander off guard. After all, since Commanders can get defensive when they don't hear what they want to hear, many of their colleagues have learned to keep their reservations about the Commander's performance to themselves.

It's important to bear in mind that while Commanders may be tough on others, they tend to be hardest on themselves. Eager to eradicate substandard performance immediately, Commanders must be reminded that they can't train themselves to treat others with patience and tolerance until they learn to handle their own learning curve with grace.

Fortunately, as they start reworking their less productive habits, most Commanders learn a powerful lesson. They learn how to give themselves credit for their most authentic accomplishments.

When the Commander Is the Boss

The good news for the Commander boss is that he or she is already in charge. Thus, the goal isn't getting the top spot—it's keeping it. While this sounds simple enough, Commanders often find that their gut reactions are better suited for combat than management. Thus, the Commander boss must remember to do the following things.

Express Appreciation Where Warranted

Because Commanders have been conditioned since childhood to perform under pressure without much "cheerleading" from their parents, they often have to learn how to make sure that the more sensitive employees on their team feel safe and appreciated. Learning the art of motivating others can be tricky for those Commanders who can't take a compliment without suspicion. While Charmers often offer encouragement for the wrong reasons—to elevate their own chances of success—Commanders, on the other hand, are hesitant to offer praise for fear that it might undermine the performance of key staff. With dedication and practice, Commanders can learn new habits that will enable them to strike the right balance so that they can express enthusiasm without fostering entitlement.

Clearly Communicate Expectations

While the Pleaser is hesitant to require subordinates to fully adhere to expectations for fear of offending, the Commander has the opposite challenge. Because of the early conditioning in their family system, it's second nature for a Commander to toe the line. Thus, they may have to cultivate a combination of tact and patience when they find themselves managing employees who don't immediately deliver what is expected. Some employees may not understand what the Commander wants the first time they are told, and others may not be listening as carefully as the boss would have hoped. When this happens, Commanders have to make sure they communicate their expectations clearly and stay mindful of the emotional trigger that can tempt them to lash out when an employee's performance is substandard.

Strengthen Your Tolerance for Curiosity and Fresh Thinking

Whether they are conscious of it or not, the Commander often comes across as the type of boss who doesn't appreciate being questioned. Because of their family experiences, Commanders operate with a sense of urgency and hate wasting time. Coming up with innovative ideas often requires unstructured brainstorming. This process can be agonizing for the Commander, who likes things to happen in an orderly and prompt fashion. If they aren't careful, Commanders may end up shutting down the best thinking of their employees because they are too preoccupied satisfying their own agenda.

Beware of Being Overly Critical of Your Best Players

Some Commanders have a tendency to be harsher with their most promising reports than with employees who they don't notice as much. This is often because, in the Commander's family system, when your performance improved, the bar was raised. This twist on tough love in the Commander family is intended to protect family members by keeping them on their toes. That said, the Commander's motivational style can confuse and sometimes alienate employees who were raised in less performance-oriented family systems.

Power Grid Case Study:
A Commander Boss Meets a Pleaser Employee

We met Steven, a Commander, and Andy, a Pleaser, in chapter 3 when we explored power plays for the Pleaser. Steven is the new division head for a large aircraft manufacturer. Andy is one of the engineers who now report to Steven.

Steven was raised in a strict Catholic family, where he internalized the classic reactions we associate with Commanders on the Power Grid. He was the second oldest of seven and grew up in a family that had rules for everything. From his earliest memories, where his father's orders were executed without question, each day began with a list of goals to be accomplished, and little time was wasted on personal chitchat.

As a result, Steven rarely let down his guard unless he was enjoying sports or playing with his children. His regimented approach to work and play became costly for Steven as his career progressed. At his previous firm, many of his reports had claimed that Steven was "difficult," and avoided dealing directly with him. Steven, and his superiors, ignored this feedback as long as the firm was growing and Steven's division remained profitable. However, when the economy contracted and key members of Steven's staff began defecting to competitors, senior management decided they needed to create a friendlier working environment to improve retention. In the process of this cultural makeover, Steven was passed over for promotion.

Nothing gets a Commander's attention like losing status. Steven felt so hurt and betrayed that he wanted to resign immediately. However, like his father before him, Steven had a secret weapon: his spouse. While Steven was the breadwinner and the disciplinarian of the household, his wife's backstage emotional support often gave him the strength he needed to stay on the battlefield. While they rarely discussed professional matters, this situation became an exception. When his wife suggested he try coaching to clarify why he had gotten derailed professionally, Steven agreed.

Throwing himself into coaching with the characteristic diligence of a Commander, Steven quickly realized that being approachable wasn't just a "soft skill" that powerful people could afford to ignore. Once he started listening more attentively and validating others, Steven's colleagues noticed. If he'd been conducting himself this way all along, his career momentum most likely wouldn't have stalled. Steven vowed that if he ever found a position that would allow him to have a fresh start, he was going to practice being a more thoughtful leader from day one.

Six months later, Steven got that chance.

His first day as the new division head for an aircraft manufacturer was challenging. Steven was in his office barely an hour when he looked up to find Andy standing in his doorway. Steven had no idea who Andy was or why he was there. Commanders rarely welcome surprise visits from people they haven't been briefed on. They don't know how to treat someone if they are unclear where that person falls in the hierarchy. Startled by Andy's impromptu appearance, Steven's first thought was, what the hell could this guy possibly be doing here? Steven asked him tersely, "Can I help you?"

Andy flinched.

Then, as his first impression with Andy hung in the balance, Steven did the best thing possible for a Commander in this situation—he paused to think before he spoke. He recognized that his first thought was an anxious reflex that fired off in his brain before he had time to assess it. The Commander's first thought frequently reflects their tendency to operate from the fear-based end of the y-axis on the Power Grid.

Thanks to his hard work in coaching, Steven had trained himself to pause and realize that what he *could* take control of was his second thought. In the past, Steven had released anxious emotional energy by letting off steam at someone else's expense. However, Steven was now able to overcome self-sabotaging behavior patterns and turn this situation around. He used the precious seconds of his strategic pause to ask himself, what do I need to do to make sure that this guy feels good about himself after he walks away from me? With this more constructive question in mind, Steven was able to relax and put his new report at ease.

Steven's coaching work had taught him to interpret clues indicating that he might be dealing with a "sensitive" employee looking for validation rather than instructions. Sizing up the situation, Steven deduced that an unfocused but eager subordinate appearing on his doorstep with little more than the desire to be noticed might as well have been wearing a neon sign labeling him as a Pleaser.

Getting passed over for promotion had taught Steven how important it was to treat sensitive employees gently and make sure they felt safe. By reflecting on his past experiences, he concluded that one upside of Pleaser employees is that they burn the midnight oil for a boss who appreciates them. The downside was that if you hurt their feelings, Pleasers could light up the office grapevine with sordid stories about you.

When logic and courtesy meet, it's a beautiful thing. In the end, Andy walked away happy that he had captured a few moments of "quality time" with his new boss, and Steven strengthened the new habits he was committed to practicing as a leader.

Many Commanders don't realize how critical it is to validate employees and make sure they feel safe. They need to remember that a little diplomacy can go a long way with all types on the grid. Some employees will find the Commander's penchant for straight talk refreshing. Other types need a gentler approach. By studying the Power Grid and applying the reconditioning process to their careers, Commanders can develop new and improved habits that will make them leaders who are respected by all types.

When the Commander Is a Peer

Commanders, who are hardwired to compete, get conditioned early in life to strive to best their peers and seek the top spot in the system. This tendency can work against Commanders who, in the grip of a blind spot, may temporarily forget that they are on the same team as their peers. It's important for Commanders to learn to balance their eagerness to advance with a conscious commitment to collaboration. Otherwise, they may inadvertently turn potential allies into adversaries.

Don't Underestimate Your Colleagues

The overly competitive Commander can get carried away by the urge to best his or her colleagues. In extreme situations, this can cause the Commander to mistake collaborative behavior on the part of a peer as a gesture of submission. Commanders whose ambition makes them overly eager to assert their superiority can leave key colleagues feeling defensive. By learning to balance their drive to advance with an understanding of the need to appreciate and support their peers, Commanders tend to rise more swiftly in their organizations and often develop more sustainable power bases.

Avoid Firing on Your Own Troops

When they are struggling with their blind spots, Commanders can fall into the trap of attacking anything that gets in their way. When they are competing internally with a peer, the Commander's gut reaction may drive them to take things too far and begin to view this peer as an enemy rather than an ally. Commanders struggling with this type of black-

and-white thinking must learn to resist the temptation to dominate people who push back on them. As Commanders learn more about their power genes and how they shape their operating style on the job, they naturally start to realize that it's often more effective to transform an opponent into an ally than it is to try to eliminate them.

Take Meaningful Risks

Commanders, hardwired to play by the rules, sometimes think following orders is the only way to merit recognition. However, if Commanders don't learn to flex their creative muscles and take meaningful risks, they can lose career momentum. This can happen to Commanders who have been carefully marching in formation for years when, suddenly, in waltzes a new colleague thinking outside the box, grabbing attention, and stealing the show. When this happens, it's more than annoying for the Commander. It can goad them into making career-killing moves such as lashing out publicly at a colleague on the job. To avoid being marginalized, Commanders need to make sure that their tendency to follow instructions isn't choking off their creativity.

Beware of Nursing a Resentment

Because they are highly competitive, Commanders hate to be thwarted by anyone for any reason. When they are dealing with a peer who moves ahead of them on the corporate ladder, a Commander struggling with their blind spots can hold a serious grudge. What's more, if a peer employs tactics with which the Commander is unfamiliar, such as a Charmer captivating superiors with his seductive powers, the Commander may perceive the situation as unfair and act out in an unproductive way. To reach their fullest professional potential, it's imperative that Commanders develop the mental and emotional agility necessary to rebound from power struggles with peers in order to collaborate successfully on future projects.

Power Grid Case Study:
The Commander Meets a Charmer

It's tough to seduce the parent in charge of a Commander-style family system. The authority figure who rules the roost in this type of family tends to be unsentimental and impressed only with results. Not surprisingly, when a Commander evaluates a peer later in life, it takes a sustained track record of both personal excellence and loyalty to the system for someone to get on their good side.

We met Ted (a Commander) and Pete (a Charmer) in chapter 5 when we explored power plays for the Charmer. You'll recall that this is the story of two men who were given the challenging assignment of coheading their firm's foreign exchange trading desk. We looked closely at the story from Pete's perspective then; let's look at Ted's now.

To understand the full scope of the challenge facing Ted in this case, it's important to consider his family background. Ted's father was a marine who started a successful construction company after being honorably discharged. His mother was a fulltime homemaker. The oldest of three boys from a disciplined military family, Ted is a team player to the core.

Ted never cared much for his colleague Pete. Their mutual distrust began brewing long before senior management decided to make them coheads of their division.

Over the years, Ted had watched Pete develop a habit of looking out for himself at the expense of other traders. When younger traders on the desk began telling Ted that Pete was grabbing full credit for deals they had worked on as well, Ted wasn't surprised. His protective instincts as a Commander looking out for his troops flared up.

Eventually, Ted got so irritated by Pete's reluctance to share credit that he voiced his complaints to the higher-ups. However, Ted quickly learned that Pete was no fool—Pete was a Charmer, and a strategic one at that. He hadn't realized that Pete had been playing golf and drinking martinis with some of the top brass. The result? Ted got chewed out for complaining about his peer.

Ted was stunned. While he had been managing the troops, his colleague Pete had been managing up. Ted reached out for coaching to help him make sense of this situation, and to figure out his next move.

Ted quickly found that he was so irritated by Pete that it felt as if he had to take a strategic pause every five minutes to avoid blowing his stack. A Commander with a great sense of humor, Ted put a roll of duct tape next to his phone shortly after he started the process. "Since I'm always on the verge of saying the wrong thing," he said wryly, "there are days when it's simpler to imagine taping my mouth shut than to try and sort through it all."

However, Ted gradually learned to focus the energy produced by his pent-up frustration into appraising what he *could* do to improve the situation. It was at this point that Ted's little pauses culminated into a giant step back and an "aha" moment about how to handle his relationship with senior management.

What Ted knew, and what senior management probably didn't want to know, was that many of Pete's most profitable trades happened because Pete was operating outside his trading limits. By endorsing a new risk management system, rather than complaining about Pete specifically, Ted would be killing two birds with one stone.

The expression on Pete's face when he learned about the risk management overhaul that Ted had gotten senior management to endorse was all Ted needed to realize he had his Charmer cohead right where he wanted him. It took all the restraint Ted had to keep from yelling, "Checkmate!" while he watched Pete fidget in his chair.

However, over the coming weeks, Pete didn't react quite as predictably as Ted might have expected. Pete swallowed his ego and got down to work.

Ted's initial draft for the risk management system focused on finding errors. After reading this draft, Pete rolled up his sleeves and made some improvements. Pete's additions transformed the system into one that would also track potential opportunities. When Ted read Pete's suggestions, he had to admit that they were visionary.

It was at this point that Ted realized his work with the Power Grid was not just about helping him grapple with problems, it was also about helping him respond constructively to opportunities. Ted realized that he was going to have to get over his resentment toward Pete and develop a positive working relationship if he wanted to maintain his own career momentum at the firm.

To both men's credit, they gradually overcame their defensiveness with each other and made their collaboration a success. They also ended up creating a risk system together that was eventually marketed across the industry and became a revenue source in its own right.

This is a particularly interesting study of peer dynamics because it highlights the innate respect that can grow between Commanders and Charmers. Both types are hardwired to win; they just go about it differently.

When the Commander Is a Subordinate

Commanders have been conditioned not to question authority figures who outrank them in the hierarchy. But while obedience can be noble, blind obedience can be career suicide. A Commander who wants to manage up effectively must learn to tell the difference.

The behavior of Commanders and that of Pleasers begin to look a lot alike when the Commander is struggling with blind spots and managing up. This is because the closer you get to the ultimate authority figure in a Commander's family system, the more your ability to advance depends on pleasing that individual any way you can. To realize their full professional potential, Commanders must recondition themselves to temper their need for approval from above with a growing ability to validate themselves from within.

When You Visit the Boss, Remember to Bring Your Brain

When senior executives I have coached encounter silent obedience from their direct reports, many of them tell me that their minds start chattering, Question me! Why don't you question me more? I hired you for your brain, not your PowerPoint skills! Many leaders love it when their reports are literally pelting them with imaginative and innovative queries. Commanders who want to manage up effectively have to speak up when they have relevant questions that will benefit the overall system. While practicing these skills takes a hard-core Commander out of his or her comfort zone, it's critical to improving performance and achieving results.

Cultivate Your Creativity

Before offering an idea or making a suggestion of any kind, Commanders operating on automatic pilot often reflect on their seniority relative to others in the system. When this ultraconservative mentality infects a critical mass of employees, innovation dries up in the organization. To rescue themselves from this rut, Commanders need to make a conscious effort to spend time doing things that get their creative juices flowing. Listening to uplifting music, appreciating art, or traveling abroad are just a few things the Commander can do to shake things up on the inside so that they can operate outside the box when it matters most.

Don't Judge Your Boss Too Harshly

As with the other quadrants, the Commander's power genes are complex and can at times elicit behavior that seems opposed to the norm. For example, despite a Commander's general reverence for authority, his or her tendency to operate with tunnel vision can kick in when he or she is evaluating a superior. This is because in the Commander's family system, leadership was a black-and-white affair where one person was firmly in charge. As a result, a Commander may have difficulty respecting a boss who seeks the approval of others and strives to keep the peace. When the boss looks weak, this pits the Commander's loyalty to their superior against their loyalty to the system and can throw them into a quandary. It's important for Commanders to learn that working for consensus isn't always spineless; sometimes it's strategic.

Push Back as a Sign of Loyalty

Since their prime directive is to hang in there and make it to the top, Commanders will usually put their heads down and silently watch a floundering boss make one mistake after another until they can eventually find a way out from under them. Commanders need to learn that speaking up when your boss is headed over the edge of a cliff isn't insubordinate. While many Commanders need to cultivate the art of disagreeing diplomatically, it's often the ultimate sign of loyalty to move beyond telling your superiors what they *want* to hear and start voicing what they *need* to hear.

Power Grid Case Study:
A Commander Challenges Authority

When it comes to tracking the market value of important art, Melinda is a warrior. A highly disciplined Commander, Melinda knows the value of economic research and hard work. The former curator of a prestigious corporate art collection, Melinda was hired by Christopher (an Inspirer) to manage his gallery and take advantage of some great buying opportunities during the economic downturn.

To fully appreciate Melinda's blind spots, it's important to understand her family background. Melinda's father, who is a highly successful money manager, was skeptical about her pursuing a career in the arts. Melinda's decision to go into the arts in spite of her father's disapproval stems from the fact that she didn't come from a pure Commander system. Her parents were divorced, and Melinda's mother, who was an Inspirer, had always encouraged her to follow her dreams.

Like many people, Melinda secretly wanted to please both her parents. From her first internship at Christie's in London to her rise to prominence managing a corporate art collection, Melinda managed to prove to her dad that she could be as successful trading art as her father had been trading securities. (Success as Melinda's father defined it, by the way, was making money.)

Melinda and Christopher had known each other in the art world for years, and when the economic downturn caused Melinda to leave her corporate position, working together seemed like a marriage made in heaven. As a status-conscious Commander, Melinda jumped at the chance to take a position where she was officially second in command because she felt this moved her up in the ranks of the art world.

It wasn't until they were huddled together in the viewing room at the top of Christopher's studio that her blind spots began to surface. Christopher, who valued innovative thinking, would begin pacing around the room, fueled by endless cups of coffee, ruminating out loud about questions such as, "But is this timeless? I know this is trendy today, but will this piece speak to the hearts of people of future generations? Would this body of work hold its own in the Met?"

Melinda, who had been conditioned to hold her tongue around superiors and follow orders, rarely expressed the strong personal reactions she had to the artwork. Her bosses in the corporate world, who assessed their purchases in primarily commercial terms, had reinforced her tendency to keep her opinions to herself. In her previous job, Melinda had been rewarded for silently getting them to consider the art more deeply and then simply buying what they wanted as cheaply as possible for them. When Christopher began pressing Melinda for her subjective opinion, her first reaction was defensive. She started to question his competence as a boss. Melinda began wondering whether

Christopher was decisive enough to build an important collection. Things were starting to get tense between them.

In the meantime, Christopher's reservations were mounting as well. Like many Inspirers, he didn't think in terms of hierarchy and approached all working relationships as if the playing field were even. Melinda's reluctance to share her point of view made him wonder whether she even had one. (We will examine Christopher's perspective more closely in chapter 9 when we discuss power plays for the Inspirer.)

Like all Commanders, Melinda was committed to succeeding at her job. She started coaching to work through the feelings of anger and frustration she felt at "never being able to do enough" to please her boss. As a dedicated Commander, since she was following his instructions carefully, she couldn't possibly imagine what else Christopher wanted from her.

As it began to dawn on her that what Christopher wanted was her opinion, Melinda was both excited and a little nervous. What if he didn't agree with her? After all, when her father didn't agree with her, he bullied Melinda into submission.

However, as Melinda began to experiment by gently questioning Christopher about some of the choices she disagreed with, she was stunned at how thrilled he was to hear her thoughts. As she began to trust that Christopher was consistently interested in her opinion, the two of them began to truly enjoy working together.

Conclusion

A self-aware Commander is a truly impressive human being. Commanders who have worked through their blind spots are able to summon unparalleled loyalty and incentivize those around them to reach higher levels of performance.

For the Commander who has developed a more balanced power

style, a gruff demeanor and "unnecessary roughness" on the job are a thing of the past. Do these men and women still get angry? You bet! However, their outbursts become few and far between. What's more, when they do occur, these displays of passion tend to be rooted in professional principles rather than personal insecurities.

CHAPTER EIGHT

Meet the Inspirer

In a world where human attention is one of our most prized commodities, Inspirers have "star power." It doesn't seem to matter whether they are standing behind a podium or standing in line for a cup of coffee; heads turn when an Inspirer is on the scene. What draws the attention of others like a magnet is the palpable sense of purpose that the Inspirer exudes. The Inspirer doesn't wander through life looking to others for a sense of direction. Inspirers trust their own instincts, and as a result, they radiate the type of self-confidence that always seems to put them in the spotlight. In our workshops, Jimmy Carter is one of the leaders often cited as exemplifying the power style of an Inspirer. Other people who are regularly mentioned for living their beliefs include Richard Branson, Margaret Mead, and Joseph Campbell.

After studying the roots of this power style, only 5 percent of our coaching population claim that they would consider themselves authentic Inspirers. For our purposes, there's a difference between an inspirational figure and an Inspirer. As we have seen in the previous chapters, inspirational figures are associated with every quadrant on the Power Grid, although Inspirers are named as such because of the unique attributes and abilities I'll describe. More specifically, an important relationship exists between Charmers and Inspirers, as both types compel our attention. To understand the difference between these diagonal quadrants on the Power Grid, bear in mind that Charmers can project an inspirational public image that diverts attention from the personal demons they struggle with in life. Inspirers, on the other hand, exhibit a consistent pattern of doing what benefits the greater good *before* taking the time to calculate what's in it for them. It's their automatic altruism that makes them stand out from the crowd.

The distinction between these power styles has important implications for Inspirers on the job. For example, many clients in competitive cultures report that they often feel forced to defend their turf or protect their professional reputations at the expense of others. Because of the ways they have been conditioned by their family systems, Inspirers are often more likely to walk away from a power struggle or even a promising job than succumb to the temptation to attack a colleague or join a catfight. Does this make them heroic, or politically naive? It depends on the situation and your point of view. One thing most people working with the Power Grid agree on is that the style of the Inspirer challenges us all to look beneath the surface and consider more deeply the ebb and flow of the emotional currents driving people's power styles.

Strengths of the Inspirer

Inspirers are easy to spot because their strengths draw us in to take a closer look. They often are larger-than-life figures because their goals can be simultaneously audacious and selfless.

Inspirers Have Charisma

If you're on the fence about whether or not thoughts can have energy, spend some time with an Inspirer. They will make you a believer.

Whether they are addressing a board of directors or performing for an audience of thousands, Inspirers operate with an innate charisma that envelops the people around them. Your best clue for identifying an Inspirer on the job is to turn down the volume on your mental chatter and check in with your feelings. The famous phrase "People don't remember what you say, they remember how they feel about what you say" was probably said first by someone describing the presentation style of an Inspirer.

Whether we intend to or not, we telegraph our self-confidence as well as our commitment to others in a myriad of nonverbal ways. The less we second-guess ourselves, the more we send signals that can act like a magnet when like-minded people pick up on the confident vocal tone, pacing, and body language that naturally accompany genuine conviction. Inspirers have been conditioned to let their thoughts and feelings flow freely. This is largely because parents in an Inspirer's family system don't force their children to suppress aspects of themselves so that the parents can remain emotionally comfortable.

Inspirers Lead by Example

Raw power infuses the energy of what an Inspirer says. This is because people who operate from this quadrant don't just pay lip service to what they believe in—they bleed for it. In a world where fewer and fewer people walk their talk, being in the presence of a genuine Inspirer can be intoxicating.

This powerful quality stems from a timeless truth that the caregivers from an Inspirer's family system frequently embrace: you have to *become* the type of human being you hope your children will want to emulate. Inspirers don't need to waste energy in their childhoods trying to figure out what's going on when Mommy and Daddy claim to respect each other but grit their teeth and glare at each other over the dinner table. Whether the Inspirer is raised in a single-parent household, a dual-parent household, or some creative variation on an extended family, this child grows up with ongoing exposure to authority figures who strive to practice what they preach.

Raised on a farm outside Plains, Georgia, President Carter was surrounded by a close-knit family who modeled the importance of independent thinking for him at an early age. In his book *The Virtues of Aging*, Carter notes that, during his childhood, reading at the table was encouraged during mealtimes: "Any discussions, of necessity, had to be more interesting than what we were reading, and were usually brief, narrowly focused and often involved controversial subjects."[1]

Carter's father, Earl, was a successful farmer and businessman, and his mother, Lillian, was a registered nurse. Carter's parents were able to hold thoughtful, contrasting, and passionate views concerning the role of segregation in the South while maintaining an even balance of power in their marriage. Growing up in this household gave Carter a unique perspective on the importance of acting on your beliefs through treating others with respect rather than just paying lip service to virtues of this kind.

The day of his inauguration in 1977, President Carter rejected the limo he was offered and chose to walk down Pennsylvania Avenue. This historic display of modeling the virtues of simplicity and honesty, rather than just talking about them, helped heal a nation that was still reeling from the betrayal of Watergate.

Inspirers Are Visionary

One reason Inspirers have an edge when it comes to innovative thinking is that their commitment to an idea or a business mission doesn't just come from the head—it comes from the heart as well. Because of Inspirers' tendency to follow what stokes their passions as well as what fuels profits, the professional causes that galvanize them often have an altruistic tone. The emotional reflexes of Inspirers guide them to support causes they consider greater than themselves. Because of their faith in and commitment to what most of us would consider beneficial causes, Inspirers have a powerful impact on the group energy of whatever system they join. What's particularly impressive is that Inspirers will often take personal risks and endure daunting obstacles to support their beliefs.

Watching their parents look out for the less fortunate and for each other conditions Inspirers to automatically consider the greater good. From their earliest memories, many Inspirers will tell you that the heroes they admired and the goals they set for themselves were aligned with helping others.

When we examine the intersection of strengths that takes place when an individual embodies both a commitment to the greater good and an ability to move the masses, we see that Inspirers bring more than vision to the table—they bring hope. Inspirers don't just consider the bigger picture, they envision ways to improve it. They also make a habit of looking for what's positive about the people and situations that surround them. As a result, Inspirers aren't just well known, they are also generally well liked.

Inspirers Treat People as Equals

We've all had these brushes with greatness: The CEO who stops in the hall to thank the janitor for keeping the place gleaming—and leaves a gleam in the eye of this employee that money can't buy. The boss who notices his secretary is having a bad day, and takes a moment to ask how she's doing rather than barking in frustration. The division head who makes sure the new employee fits in with the rest of the team rather than leaving this recruit to sink or swim. Regardless of the seniority of someone who exhibits these kinds of reactions, people who witness this kind of behavior know they are in the presence of a genuine leader. This quality is instinctual for Inspirers. They have the common touch.

While Commanders and Inspirers both gravitate to working with groups, Commanders have a hierarchical approach, and Inspirers see the world as more of a level playing field. Because Inspirers trust that good ideas can come from anyone, regardless of their seniority, they deal easily with groups and listen carefully to input from colleagues at all levels in their system. On the job, an Inspirer is likely to be as respectful toward the receptionist as he or she is toward the CEO.

Due to their respect for and ease with people from all walks of life, Inspirers exhibit behavior that motivates people around them to share their enthusiasm. What's more, people who are in the presence of an Inspirer often find that the ability to relax and think more freely is contagious. This makes Inspirers appealing to others on an emotional as well as an intellectual level. It can also make them wildly popular both as managers and as mentors.

Inspirer Blind Spots

The visionary passion of the Inspirer, which is their greatest strength, can also sow the seeds of their professional demise. When an Inspirer gets so focused on the big picture that they miss the personal agendas that may be driving their colleagues, and the tactical details that may be driving their organizations, a promising career can get derailed. Inspirers must guard against getting so swept away by their innate enthusiasm that they forget the importance of a sound political strategy when it comes to operating effectively within a large organization.

Inspirers Can Be Politically Naive

Inspirers can get blindsided if they approach projects by being so focused on the bird's-eye view of the potential that they miss what's lurking in the weeds. One of the main things lurking in the weeds is often people whose motives are less noble than their own. By overlooking the personal agendas driving other types on the grid, Inspirers can experience an organizational backlash that scuttles some of their best ideas. When this happens, it's not just the Inspirer's career that starts sinking, their organization often takes a big hit as well.

As with many Inspirers, Carter's outspoken and visionary nature cast him as a political outsider. As the governor of Georgia, Carter was known for regularly going over the heads of the assembly to get his programs passed. During his presidency, Carter focused on supporting legislation that cut the pork barrel projects that Congress loved. Like many Inspirers who try to fly above the personal agendas of ambitious colleagues, Carter became a political target for some of his peers. With only a fragile hold on his own party's support, he faced a backlash from his political opponents that left many of his programs stranded in committee on Capitol Hill and caused his moral standards to be called into question amid financial scandals.

Another symptom of an inspirer's political naïveté is a failure to recognize when their success and popularity is met with envy by superiors. It's a form of tunnel vision when they continue to pursue a passionate campaign, never pausing to appease the jealous colleagues whom they need in support of their efforts.

Turning a blind eye to the political agendas of others can put Inspirers on the endangered species list. People operating from other quadrants often "sense" a certain power in the Inspirer that they don't quite understand. Instead of being drawn to support Inspirers, individuals who are deeply entrenched in their own agendas may have the automatic reaction to eliminate anyone powerful enough to deflect attention away from them. During senior management reorganizations, the power plays that people from other quadrants will resort to when they covet the popularity of an Inspirer can feel like the opening day of hunting season in a game preserve. Thus, for the sake of their professional survival, it's important for Inspirers to study the power plays employed by people operating from other quadrants on the grid.

Inspirers Have Trouble Dealing with Red Tape

It's not uncommon to see Inspirers grow weary of the bureaucracy in a large organization and choose to strike out on their own. Depending on their aptitude for entrepreneurship, they may face many of the same frustrations in the new organization they have created and end up feeling like victims of their own success.

From their earliest memories in their family system, Inspirers learned to value freedom. They like the freedom to manage their own time without restrictions. They like the freedom to brainstorm openly. They like the freedom to express their feelings spontaneously. Here's the rub: the desire to be part of an organization or movement that is greater than yourself and the longing to feel independent and free of constraints often pull people in different directions. These sometimes diametrically opposed urges can, in extreme cases, create what feels like an internal civil war in the psyche of the Inspirer.

By studying other types on the Power Grid, the Inspirer can learn some valuable lessons about tolerance and perspective when it comes to working with others. Whether they realize it or not—and our less conscious reactions become blind spots precisely because we *don't* recognize them—when Inspirers vote with their feet and walk away, their actions are screaming their dissatisfaction even when they don't articulate their complaints. Through studying different power styles, the Inspirer can learn how to manage small conflicts more effectively so they don't escalate into exit scenarios.

A central skill that's required in large business structures that can confound Inspirers is the need to manage underperforming employees. Inspirers tend to get on the fast track early in their careers and stay there. One reason for this is that they are generally easy to manage. Because they have been raised in a family system where they were given plenty of room to express themselves authentically, Inspirers rarely need excessive compliments or reprimands to stay on track. However, the larger a particular system is, the more likely it is that an Inspirer will need to manage less self-motivated employees. Here's another area where studying people who operate with different power styles can help the Inspirer work effectively within a larger business structure.

Inspirers Ignore Details in Favor of the Big Picture

Inspirers do not just think outside the box, they frequently ignore the box altogether. When they do this, Inspirers may overlook critical details that can derail their best intentions. The most elegant strategy must be practical if it's going to be successfully executed. To keep their ideas commercially viable, Inspirers need to get feedback from other types on the grid to make sure they have considered the nuts and bolts of what is required to make their vision a reality.

Steve Jobs is a business leader who has been the subject of intense speculation in our Power Grid discussions on the Inspirer. Because of his consistent ability to drive innovation, some participants consider him to be an Inspirer.

One thing that Jobs can teach us is that even the best innovative thinkers can get into trouble when they focus so heavily on their vision that they overestimate the abilities of other key players to manage the details of execution. In Jobs's case, this pitfall came to light when AT&T, the exclusive wireless carrier for the iPhone, ran into capacity problems that prevented Apple's customers from enjoying the benefits that the original version of the iPhone was intended to provide. Although Jobs managed the situation, his predicament at the time revealed that turning a vision into reality isn't just an exercise in strategic supremacy, it's a tactical and collaborative adventure as well.

In addition to exhibiting a strong preference for the big picture and a willingness to sacrifice attention to detail, Inspirers can fall into the trap of surrounding themselves with other high-level, big-picture thinkers. As far as an Inspirer is concerned, everyone on the team is equal and deserves to be making important decisions. Yet, in order to execute their vision, Inspirers must build diverse teams that contain enough on-the-ground expertise to be responsible for the tactical and practical details.

Inspirers Can Risk Burnout

I'll never forget telling one beloved Inspirer who was struggling with an overload of challenges at his organization and considering leaving, "You can't help anyone here if you don't have a pulse."

The head of HR referred to this Inspirer as the "cultural glue" that was keeping some of the most talented performers from walking out the door of this prominent financial services firm. In feedback meetings, otherwise cynical and savvy traders were telling me things like, "I'd go to Iraq for this guy . . . I'd throw myself on a live grenade for this guy . . . I trust this man with my family's financial future." This Inspirer was everyone's favorite mentor, senior management's moral compass, and the first call most people made in the firm when a difficult client was on the line. Hey, no pressure, right?

Sadly, one sign that you're dealing with an Inspirer can be the dark circles under their eyes. While it's commendable to watch an Inspirer passionately work for a cause they believe in, the backstage view of this heroic performance can be daunting if the Inspirer's schedule becomes so demanding that his or her health and family relationships come under pressure. This happens when the Inspirer's commitment to helping others begins to eclipse his or her commitment to personal balance.

An Inspirer's Family Background

It's important to note that the two-parent heterosexual household, where parents stay married for life, is not considered as typical as it was when Salvador Minuchin, R. D. Laing, and Virginia Satir were developing their theories about family systems dynamics in the 1960s and 1970s. Thus, any framework for studying the impact of family dynamics on job performance later in life would be incomplete without recognizing the wide range of single-parent and extended family systems that are prevalent in our culture. This issue comes to the forefront naturally when we study the family system of Inspirers. That's because in the Inspirer system, the caregivers are often (although certainly not always) highly self-actualized as individuals and less bound by any specific traditions and norms that might limit their ability to live into the idealized vision they have for themselves. Whether they are adopted, raised in single-parent homes, or even raised by parents who have remained good friends following a divorce, Inspirers report also that their caregivers by and large treat each other with respect—thus giving some young Inspirers a beginning that (compared with that of some other power types) is less burdened by painful or codependent family dynamics. The important point here isn't whether or not an Inspirer comes from a nontraditional family structure; it's the fact that they are raised by authority figures who are predisposed to try to work through domestic conflicts head-on or else find a way to gracefully exit the union. They tend not to feel bound by contract to settle, or remain in a marriage or relationship that is not functioning. As a result, when Inspirers are faced with conflicts on the job, they are more likely than other types on the grid to leave a system they consider dysfunctional.

The structure of a healthy family system is built on the foundation of the caregivers' ability to respect each other and share power maturely. This foundation of mutual respect among authority figures is actively modeled in the day-to-day interactions that take place in an Inspirer's family system. Thus, children raised in an Inspirer system rarely have their precious energy drained by needing to adapt to power struggles taking place between their caregivers.

How do the authority figures in an Inspirer's family avoid the petty power struggles that plague so many of us? In an Inspirer system, the caregivers tend to define themselves as individuals rather than basing their sense of identity on the role they play in the system. The secret is that the caregivers in this family draw energy from supporting a cause that they feel is greater than themselves. For some this is a form of artistic expression, and for others it may be a commitment to politics or even to spiritual growth. Whatever this higher calling is, it fulfills each individual parent's need for personal meaning to such an extent that they don't need to drain each other's energy to feel alive.

It's worth noting that while the balance of power in the family systems of both the Commander and the Inspirer can be heavily influenced by the caregivers' commitment to a larger cultural system, an important distinction exists between the types of values these two systems foster within children. In the Commander's family, both the family and the larger system that this family aligns itself with operate hierarchically. In contrast, both the Inspirer's family system and any larger cultural systems their family embraces tend to have less formal rules and fewer requirements for conformity.

In fact, the need for conformity is so low in the families of some Inspirers that each parent often feels free to devote his or her efforts to supporting different causes. For example, the mother of an Inspirer may channel her efforts into educational reform, while her husband finds that his passion is composing music. Thus, while time and resources must be negotiated in all families, the Inspirer system is spared many of the power struggles that take place when one parent tries to force the other to adapt to his or her priorities.

Parents from Inspirer family systems must ponder a critical question: how much freedom is too much freedom? Without a baseline of discipline, Inspirers risk becoming so nonconformist that they don't learn to plan, overlook details, and can't work collaboratively within any larger system.

In his fabulously witty and practical book, *Get Out of My Life, But First Could You Drive Me and Cheryl to the Mall?* child psychologist Anthony Wolf explores the pros and cons of changes in the structure of the relationship between parents and children when he writes:

Old-style respect is gone. We have entered a new era in child rearing. Perhaps the old way was easier and more pleasant, but it is gone. Nostalgia is acceptable, but that style of parenting also had a flaw, in my opinion. It was based in part on establishing fear. Creating fear as an explicit child-raising practice has had some bad consequences. It can breed anger and resentment. It can intimidate and cause the intimidated to lose confidence in themselves. Perhaps worst of all, it tells children that in the service of getting what one wants, fear and intimidation are necessary and acceptable in everyday life.[2]

Wolf has some refreshingly practical advice that goes to the heart of the parenting style that takes place in the Inspirer system. He suggests that parents, caregivers, and authority figures on the job all need to "grow up" and learn to respond with maturity rather than frustration when they are emotionally triggered. This tends to happen naturally in an Inspirer system because self-actualized caregivers in this type of family system are able to respond to challenges from their kids with a combination of personal confidence and humility.

Wolf describes the parenting style that children often experience in an Inspirer system when he writes:

The first step is to accept a child's right to say what he or she has to say no matter how stupid or unreasonable. You don't have to listen to all of it, you can leave whenever you want, but you respect their right to say it. Then you say what you have to say, and are not blown away by the inevitable response. This kind of parenting earns respect. It's the strength *not* to descend to the teenager's level of name-calling, when they would lose respect for you. It's the strength to walk away . . . You need confidence and not the confidence that you are always making the right decision—nobody can do that—or that you are always in control of the kid—nobody can even come close to doing *that*. Rather, you need the confidence that you are the right person for the job, and that your efforts are definitely not in vain.[3]

Don't think Wolf's advice is only helpful for parents. The number of senior executives I've worked with who have read Wolf's book and found it a valuable field guide for interacting with immature employees is substantial. And the relevant point, then, is that the freedom that helps shape Inspirers in so many critical ways could also backfire and make them less effective individuals and employees.

What do Inspirers who grow up exposed to emotionally independent caregivers do with all the extra energy that's freed from the power struggles that can take place in less tolerant family systems? Our work with Inspirers indicates that this free psychic space often gets filled by an astounding amount of creativity.

Inspirers are often inventive early in life. By the time they headed for college, several of the Inspirers I have coached told me that they had already designed products ranging from a sound-recording device that is now used throughout the music industry to a successful line of designer clothing. Over the past couple of years, an increasing number of graduate students I have spoken with at colleges across the country have told me that they identify with the Inspirer power style. Many of them have gone on to say that they have begun to view working in a large organization as a stepping-stone to starting their own business where they can focus on what will add value for others without needing to deal with the cumbersome politics that they read about daily in the business press. This trend may be due to the fact that young people have witnessed a great deal of instability in some of our most high-profile business organizations over the last few years. These comments may also reflect the fact that Inspirers rarely think in terms of careers. Inspirers are more likely to focus on visions or causes.

Some Inspirers are drawn to the arts because this is such a straightforward outlet for self-expression. What's more, Inspirers tend to get support for their artistic ambitions early in life. For example, a young person who shows an aptitude for music in an Inspirer family system often gets an instrument and music lessons. In a different type of family system, this same child might be advised to study something more practical and be handed a math book. Those Inspirers who find themselves drawn to more traditional areas of business often approach the world of commerce from an artistic point of view. These patterns stem from the fact that in an Inspirer system, professional goals were never just monetary. These types of families encourage young people to courageously follow their dreams.

The Inspirer in Transition

Why would a company ever risk losing a talented and well-intentioned Inspirer? You'd think organizations would hang on to these employees any way they could.

Reviewing the career histories of Inspirers who ended up surprised by a pink slip gives us all an important lesson in the importance of stamina, boundaries, and good conflict resolution skills.

Inspirers rarely fight, and they avoid turf wars. This is because while their family experiences may have conditioned them to have endless vision in terms of how to improve a situation, they didn't get much trench warfare experience in how to grapple with power struggles that have less to do with what's right and more to do with what's expedient. The absence of corporate survival skills can be detrimental to Inspirers and sometimes tragic for their organizations.

Another thing that can plunge Inspirers into a transitional quandary is that they often quit on a whim. When they don't like the way things are going in an organization, Inspirers tend to be more likely to vote with their feet than dig their heels in. Don't let the Inspirer's focus on the greater good lull you into thinking these talented men and women aren't demanding. The difference comes in *what* they demand, and Inspirers demand leadership that merits their respect. Inspirers rarely lose faith in the mission—but they often lose faith in the senior management team when they don't walk their talk. Remember, Inspirers are conditioned to practice what they preach.

If you are trying to hire Inspirers, bear in mind that the personal integrity of your senior management team will mean as much to them as the salary of the position. While they are often modest about it, Inspirers take their power seriously and won't lend it to causes they don't respect. They innately understand that their presence will help shape the corporate culture they choose to support. They also understand that their values, self-esteem, and quality of life will be affected by spending a segment of their lives as part of any culture.

When an organization loses its way culturally, it can be hard to hold on to the Inspirers that may be keeping the firm together. This is because you can't rent an Inspirer; you have to lead them. If you aren't mindful of how your key employees treat each other and you allow an atmosphere of toxic competition to fester, your Inspirers won't protest—they will simply leave. Once an Inspirer has decided to go, it takes more than money to get him or her to reconsider.

If an Inspirer doesn't see that the leaders in their organization are modeling the values they expect from their employees, they may stay in their positions for the short term out of loyalty to the people who report to them, but they will eventually walk.

Losing an Inspirer has ramifications that organizations often don't understand until he or she is gone. The departure of an Inspirer is usually a powerful example of the fact that not *all* employees are expendable. The motivational impact of losing a critical Inspirer can bring an organization or department to its knees and force cultural change.

The good news is that when updating the résumé becomes inevitable, many Inspirers are happy and surprised to discover that they are spoiled for choice. While people from other quadrants are furiously thumbing through their Rolodexes and arranging lunch meetings with headhunters, it's not unusual to find the Inspirer's phone ringing off the hook. What makes Inspirers so popular? The reason is both simple and powerful. Rather than approaching the world of work with a "what can you do for me?" attitude, the Inspirer is often focused on what they can do for others.

An Inspirer in Action

Leslie is an Inspirer whose popularity in the business community made her a political target. A partner at a prominent law firm, Leslie is a tireless advocate for women's rights. The older of two children, Leslie comes from a literary family. Her parents are both professors. Her father is a historian who has written several popular books on the Civil War, and her mother has a doctorate in English and specializes in the romantic poets. Leslie's little brother, Matt, is an entrepreneur who runs his own television production studio and has made some widely respected independent films.

When Leslie was growing up, dinnertime at her home was often a celebration. Leslie was exposed to a parade of artists, activists, and academics who ended up at her parents' numerous parties, laughing around the table and sharing ideas late into the night.

From her earliest memories, Leslie had been encouraged to follow her heart and to think for herself. The result of this Renaissance upbringing was that Leslie became fascinated with protecting the rights of the less fortunate and decided that she wanted to be an attorney. Both of her parents, who just wanted her to do whatever excited her, made sure nothing got in the way of her favorite TV show: Perry Mason.

Leslie made top grades in college, played varsity tennis, and managed to get early acceptance to Harvard Law School. Upon graduation, she joined a top corporate law firm and began working her way up. Not only did Leslie become the first woman partner at her firm, she also became the youngest partner in her firm's history.

By anyone's standards, Leslie was a superstar. This was particularly true when it came to championing working women. When a diversity conference needed a high-profile woman to motivate the next generation, they called Leslie. When young women at her firm needed a mentor for career perspective, they called Leslie. When hardworking women in the industry needed senior-level support to get through a professional tight spot, they called Leslie. Whether the request was big or small, Leslie almost always managed to respond. Over time, Leslie had amassed the type of power that comes from being a well-known supporter of a cause that is considered important to the system.

Leslie's concern for the challenges facing working women hit close to home when one of her colleagues, Charlotte, needed flextime to balance her professional commitments with the mounting demands of caring for a developmentally challenged son. Because Charlotte had been a top producer for the firm, Leslie was stunned when several of her fellow partners were reluctant to approve flextime for their division.

When Inspirers believe in a cause, they will walk through fire to support it. Fueled by her passion for supporting the rights of working women, Leslie tapped into the same emotional energy that had inspired her to fight for the underdog when she had started reading about political activism as a child.

In the grip of her passion for positive change, Leslie made the decision to go over the heads of the partners at her level and to take her case directly to Andy, the managing partner of the firm. This turned out to be a costly political misstep.

Andy, who was caught off guard by Leslie's impulsive appeal, found himself flustered—agreeing to support Leslie's demands more because he feared a lawsuit than because he agreed with her position.

Because Leslie had forgotten to go through the proper channels, Andy saw Leslie's spontaneity as unprofessional rather than courageous. What's more, whenever Leslie's efforts on the diversity front landed her in the media, Andy secretly got a little jealous. Inspirers must remain mindful of the fact that they may make their colleagues (or even their boss) envious when they are consistently the center of attention. In feedback meetings, we later discovered that Andy was frequently fuming and asking, "How does *she* always manage to grab the spotlight when *I'm* the head of the firm?"

Over the course of the next few months, a series of meetings began to take place behind Leslie's back. The agenda items: to manage the morale of the remaining women at the firm while managing Leslie out of the organization.

Leslie, who had been so focused on supporting the women in the firm that she had no idea any of this was going on, was stunned when she found out that she was being downsized. She had no idea that her behavior could be perceived as threatening by Andy and others at her firm. Like many Inspirers, she was oblivious to the fact that the industrywide attention she drew might foster envy among some colleagues. Specifically, she failed to realize that her impulsive behavior could so unnerve the Charmers and Commanders working around her. For example, before they understand their blind spots, those Charmers who are driven by the need to feel superior may lash out at an Inspirer whose star is on the rise. Commanders, who often feel justified in punishing anyone who steps outside their role in the hierarchy, can also feel triggered to trip up an overzealous Inspirer. When the urge to "save the day" gets overwhelming, Inspirers often find themselves in the danger zone. Getting wrapped up in the drama of corporate life can happen to the best of us. Sadly, when Inspirers get swept away by how much others need them, and forget the importance of operating strategically when dealing with a large organization, it can be a career killer.

Leslie reached out for coaching to make sense of it all. Through studying the power style of the Commander, Leslie was able to prepare herself to revisit the topic with Andy in a more logical and less emotional manner. At precisely the moment that a less confident person might have hemmed and hawed, Leslie's innate self-confidence as an Inspirer came through, and she was determined to face her challenge directly.

After reviewing the power style of the Charmer, Leslie caught on quickly that Andy's decision to let her go was rooted in emotions that he might prefer to ignore. While Andy would have liked a private meeting so that he could put the spin he chose on the situation, Leslie knew it was important to have a witness present. Leslie called Becky in human resources and asked whether, for the good of the firm, Becky could arrange a meeting where the two of them could go together to have a conversation with Andy.

After thanking Andy for taking the meeting, Leslie looked him in the eye and apologized for the lack of professional restraint she had exhibited in terms of how she had handled her reaction to Charlotte's situation. She told him, flatly, that if she could turn back time, she would have approached the matter more diplomatically.

It's hard to ignore the truth when the person delivering the message is grounded enough to speak with humility. While Andy had been squirming in his seat when the meeting began, he stopped glancing at his watch and began to listen carefully as Leslie succinctly and dispassionately explained how many of the top-performing women at the firm felt subtly marginalized when it came to getting paid and getting ahead. This time, Leslie wasn't emotional. She presented some compelling examples to show Andy how it wasn't in the firm's best financial interest to let this trend continue.

When an Inspirer taps into his or her innate communication skills, it's remarkable to watch how people react to the power of truth in action. By the end of the meeting, Andy had made up his mind to take diversity much more seriously. Feeling more than a little guilty about his own impulsive reaction to the situation, he also ended up giving Leslie a fabulous job reference that helped keep her career on track.

Conclusion

Because of their unrehearsed approach to life, Inspirers have an advantage when it comes to innovative thinking. They will ask questions out loud that people whose power genes predispose them to censor their ideas and feelings can't even formulate in their own minds. Why are we in this business in the first place? Should we face the fact that this client base has simply dried up? Why don't we try something completely different? Inspirers have an uncanny knack for perceiving what's vital for the future survival of a business. One reason some Inspirers get ahead and stay ahead is that they are able to spot patterns that shape the big picture and have a lasting impact on any system.

We all have a stake in protecting the Inspirers within our organizations and in nurturing the strengths of the Inspirer within ourselves. Finding the right marriage of authenticity and political savvy is the key to helping the Inspirer develop a more balanced power style.

CHAPTER NINE

Inspirer Power Plays

Inspirers are the rugged individuals of corporate America, the pioneering thinkers in academia, and the visionary artists who create the symbols that embody our cultural experience.

Although they are motivated to do what's best for the group, Inspirers are such independent thinkers that they often don't view challenges through the lens of the "group mind." While the tendency to think outside the box boosts the creative potential of many Inspirers, it makes implementation a struggle for them. Until they embrace the pros and cons of working within an organization in an evenhanded way, Inspirers can find themselves floundering when it comes to *any* type of management: managing up, managing down, managing across, or even managing themselves.

The paradox of wanting to help a group that's often lagging behind them conceptually is both the root of the Inspirer's talent and the source of their potential demise. To realize the full scope of their creative abilities, Inspirers need to learn how to leverage the structures they work in rather than rejecting the limitations of a particular system prematurely. Inspirers also need to appreciate that the personal agendas of people who operate from other quadrants can present more than an impediment to progress. Resistance from people who see the world differently from them can offer the Inspirer clues to the tactical dimensions of a challenge that they may not have considered previously.

When the Inspirer Is the Boss

The Inspirer has come from a family system where they were encouraged to candidly express their full range of thoughts and feelings to authority figures. However, it takes more than innovative thinking to run a successful business. It's critical for Inspirers in senior management to be surrounded by people from other quadrants who will balance their sense of vision with the practicality necessary to keep the firm commercially viable.

Inspirers don't care what your title is; they care about what you can do to help the organization. Thus, the underlying tone established by Inspirers is one where it feels as if they are always dealing with peers—even when the Inspirer is the boss. As warm and collaborative as this can be, it presents a problem when someone needs to be held accountable for the detail work. Inspirers should bear in mind that if they don't sometimes "subordinate their subordinates," they won't have anyone looking after the details that keep an organization running smoothly.

Successful Inspirers often find it helpful to surround themselves with Pleasers who have an eye for the administrative and tactical details that they tend to miss. Still, once they have identified and hired some talented Pleasers for their team, the Inspirer must resist the temptation to turn staff meetings into brainstorming sessions. If they don't let their subordinates play their designated role, something may fall between the cracks.

Keep an Eye on the Politics Brewing Beneath You

There's an argument to be made that a boss who isn't managing the politics within his or her department isn't managing at all. Some Inspirers, particularly those in large organizations, are naively oblivious to the fact that they have subordinates who will resort to things that they wouldn't dream of to further a personal agenda. The Inspirer who wants to run an effective team can't have his or her head in the clouds when it comes to monitoring the personal dynamics between staff members. For a department to run effectively, the staff must know that power struggles and turf wars will be resolved in a professional and straightforward manner and won't degenerate into informal popularity contests. While many Inspirers would rather fly safely above the fray when tension is brewing in the ranks, a good manager can't afford to ignore these squabbles. The boss must have his or her finger on the pulse of what's happening between key staff members to be prepared to coach them through the rough spots so they can work together effectively.

Get Feedback from Outside Your Fan Club

Inspirers are so likeable that colleagues may avoid telling them the hard truths they need to hear. When it comes to Inspirers in senior management, the hard truth often has something to do with ways that their visionary zeal is causing them to miss commercial opportunities. What's more, it's often the Inspirer's staff that gets wind that something's wrong in Camelot long before it dawns on the Inspirer boss. Because of this, Inspirers need to keep company with people who *haven't* been fans of their work. While the Inspirer often has to coax colleagues and staff members to share negative feedback, it's worth it. Even if a complaint is coming from someone who has an ax to grind, and their perspective is distorted, this will still help the Inspirer understand how their efforts may be perceived by people who don't share their vision.

Create Incentives for Innovation

Hiring other types on the grid is one thing, but managing them so that you get what you need most from them is quite another. To do this, Inspirers have to be sure that their system is structured to reward subordinates for creative thinking and for speaking up. If an Inspirer boss doesn't take the time to reward creativity, key team members are likely to stay within their own comfort zone until they see the payoff for intellectual elbow grease. Inspirer bosses frequently overlook this simple point because no one ever had to incentivize them to innovate—they do this naturally.

Inspirers should let their direct reports know point blank that they want to hear their ideas and that they will be rewarded for innovative thinking. This can require a sustained effort because some subordinates, Commanders in particular, can be so eager to act that getting them to reflect on what they are doing and *why* they are doing it can be challenging. Remember, Commanders aren't conditioned to ask questions; they are conditioned to execute orders.

Create Structures as Incentives

Formalizing incentive programs and enforcing consequences can seem foreign to the Inspirer whose family system prized freedom of expression so much that they learned to avoid structure for fear of stifling creativity. But the Inspirer's direct reports may need explicit direction in order to fulfill their potential. Putting thoughtful performance evaluation, compensation, and succession-planning structures in place can help establish the needed goals and guidelines for subordinates. It will also help the Inspirer's boss see that his or her feet are solidly on the ground in terms of meeting the challenges of managing a diverse team.

Power Grid Case Study:
The Inspirer Managing a Commander

Christopher is an art gallery owner and an Inspirer. His father was a founding partner of one of the world's best-known advertising agencies. His mother, a former model, was an active philanthropist. Both of his parents were passionate about politics. Because of the ongoing fund-raisers held in his home, Christopher grew up surrounded by many of America's most prominent business leaders, artists, and politicians. Like many Inspirers, Christopher developed the desire to make a lasting mark on American culture.

As we learned in chapter 7, Christopher recently hired Melinda (a self-identified Commander) to make some strategic purchases for his gallery during the market downturn. When Melinda agreed to work for Christopher, he was elated. He had dedicated much of his career to supporting new artists, and Melinda's previous job as a corporate curator had empowered her to purchase the work of rising stars they had both admired.

However, once Melinda became his direct report, Christopher couldn't hide his disappointment when she began dodging his direct questions about how she "felt" about a piece of art by hiding behind a spreadsheet analysis of its market value. One day, Christopher simply couldn't hide his frustration when Melinda started spouting numbers at him. "Damn it, Melinda!" he exploded. "This collection is as much a personal mission for me as it is a business. Could you try to reference something a little deeper than money once in a while!"

By the look on her face, Christopher could see that Melinda was stricken. An inevitable mismatch of performance expectations takes place when an Inspirer manages down to a Commander. The heart of this mismatch comes from how they each learned to operate around authority figures. The Inspirer, who pays little attention to hierarchy, longs for the type of sounding board one finds in a trusted peer. In contrast, the Commander has been conditioned to follow instructions and question authority as little as possible.

For an Inspirer like Christopher to get what he needed from this important hire, he was going to have the take the time necessary to clarify his expectations in terms of how they approached the process of selecting art. Commanders will do whatever it takes to please the boss, but they aren't mind readers. As they worked together to establish an evaluation process they could both understand, Melinda began to meet and in some cases exceed his expectations.

If Inspirers want a Commander to stop operating on automatic pilot and bring more originality to work, they are going to have to incorporate some type of structure that consistently reminds the Commander that fresh thinking is a performance requirement. To convince any type of employee that they are serious about making innovative thinking part of their required job description, Inspirers need to create financial incentives tied to their subordinates' creative efforts.

The Inspirer as a Peer

Peer relationships come so naturally to Inspirers that they tend to treat everyone they work with as equals. As we have seen, one inherent danger here is that as they rise within the hierarchy of their system, Inspirers' tendencies to dismiss the importance of rank can make them a political target for Charmers and Commanders. Before Inspirers have worked through their blind spots, some Charmers and Commanders may try to position themselves as senior to the Inspirer. Inspirers must remember that when jostling with peers for the next top spot, the less self-aware Charmers and Commanders may be tempted to elbow anyone aside who looks like an easy target.

My work with Inspirers has taught me that noble intentions, widespread popularity, and even celebrity can't fully protect an Inspirer from competitive peers within his or her system. Inspirers who hope to maintain a sustainable power base must remain mindful of the personal agendas driving their peers.

Identify Jealous Colleagues and Share the Spotlight

Inspirers have to remember that their natural charisma and the attention it attracts may spark a backlash from insecure colleagues. A jealous colleague can become a dangerous colleague. Feeling eclipsed by an Inspirer can bring out the dark side of envious peers. On the job, this dark side often drives the green-eyed peer to places where they feel they can express their hostility anonymously. This can be the office grapevine, where they may drop complaints and unfavorable comments. Granted, this is the reputational equivalent of road rage. In a perfect world we'd all ignore it. Unfortunately, it's not a perfect world, and it can still hurt the unaware Inspirer.

How can you, as an Inspirer, insulate yourself from stealth attacks by envious peers? Remember to share the spotlight with your colleagues whenever possible. Also, be sure you take the time to carefully consider the contribution your peers are making and to run this up the flagpole to senior management when appropriate. The best defense against being stabbed in the back is to be known far and wide as an enthusiastic advocate of others. To the extent that you remember to do this, you are less likely to become a target when your popularity is on the rise.

Don't Lose Sight of Commercial Practicalities

Make sure your peers understand how your thought process can benefit them commercially. Don't think that they will give you the benefit of the doubt on this. Many types on the grid may need you to connect the dots on this for them because they don't share your priorities. For example, if one of your peers is a Charmer and they don't see how your ideas will benefit their bottom line, they may secretly find a way to manage you out if they think you are in their way.

In many business situations, the administrative details that Inspirers tend to gloss over can be at the heart of the commercial point. Because of their tendency to overlook details, Inspirers will often innocently allow peers to take control of the administrative aspects of projects while they ponder the big picture. I've seen this misstep undermine the power base of some talented Inspirers. It's not uncommon for the Inspirer's colleagues to use their knowledge and control of administrative details to maneuver themselves ahead of the Inspirer and grab credit for any success associated with a key project.

Accept That Some People Refuse to Think Outside the Box

Some people are determined to do things the way they've always been done, for a variety of reasons. They don't want to think that hard; the status quo is profitable for them personally; they are risk averse—the list goes on and on. For example, when the Inspirer is managing across to a Commander, they are dealing with a peer who usually doesn't like to think outside the box, because many Commanders don't see taking the time to brainstorm as practical. Commanders are action oriented. Since many Commanders aren't comfortable unless they are in perpetual motion, pausing to think through complex issues can be emotionally agonizing for them. To work productively with peers from other quadrants on the grid, the Inspirer must always bear in mind that their peers see the world differently and have other priorities.

Don't Spend Too Much Time with the Cheerleaders

Even when peers agree with you wholeheartedly, it's still not always smooth sailing. Enjoy a supportive sounding board, but make sure you and the peers who naturally share your vision don't lose sight of commercial realities. While sharing a sense of vision with peers may give you an energy boost, you both may need a reality check from other quadrants in order to bring you back down to earth. If not, both of you risk getting carried away with your ideas of how things *should* work and missing crucial details in terms of how to *do* the work in the current environment.

Power Grid Case Study: An Inspirer and His Pleaser Peer

Paul is an Inspirer, and Dave is a Pleaser. These two manage across to one another as directors in the information technology division of a large investment bank. They both report to a new boss, another Inspirer, named Jeff.

When Paul was growing up as an Inspirer, one of the unspoken rules from his childhood was that talent and professional advancement always took a back seat to maintaining solid relationships with close family and friends. Paul recalls numerous family functions from his childhood where his parents entertained a mix of people ranging from celebrated academics to out-of-work musicians. By the end of the evening, they were all singing together under the stars around the fire pit—regardless of age or social standing.

Like many Inspirers, Paul grew up less interested in where someone fell in the hierarchy of any organization than in what that individual could contribute to helping the system advance. His easygoing manner always made Paul's superiors feel free to crack jokes and speak their mind around him without worrying that Paul would become preoccupied with how their relationship might boost his career.

A chance encounter at a local coffee bar sparked an informal friendship between Paul and the group's new boss, Jeff. As they were both Inspirers, Jeff responded positively to Paul's creative thought process and soon began dropping by Paul's office on a regular basis.

While Paul wasn't counting how many times Jeff stopped by, Paul's colleague Dave was practically charting these visits. The fact that the boss kept spending time with Paul and not bonding with him was driving Dave crazy. Behind Paul's back, Dave began insinuating that Paul might be undermining others to position himself with the boss.

What the Inspirer has to bear in mind is that a jealous Pleaser can hurt their professional reputation. If they don't get the attention they want in a constructive way, Pleasers will often manufacture a way to get the attention by less-than-legitimate means. Dave started dealing with his frustration by complaining through the office grapevine.

There are a few truths in life you can almost always count on. The sun will rise tomorrow, the law of gravity will hold, and when you start gossiping about people, they will eventually find out.

When Paul realized how and why he had become the brunt of office gossip, it seemed unbelievable to him that Dave would care so much about a few casual encounters with the boss. However, once he grasped that Dave was so preoccupied with the matter, Paul was smart enough to take action promptly to ease the situation.

The next time Jeff stepped into Paul's office, Paul made a point of inviting Dave into the conversation. Paul also began sending e-mails to Jeff and to his other colleagues to compliment people who did good work. Paul did this to leverage the power of grapevine chatter to restore his reputation as a supportive and trustworthy colleague.

The main thing to bear in mind when you are an Inspirer managing across to a Pleaser is that he or she is going to notice many political signals that you miss. While the Inspirer is focused on big-picture issues, the Pleaser is hardwired to spot the nuances of who appears to be most popular with senior managers. If you sense jealousy or discord among your colleagues, don't sweep it under the rug. Take control of the group dynamic promptly and positively.

When the Inspirer Is a Subordinate

As we have seen, when an Inspirer is focused on what they consider to be a worthy cause, they can tend to overlook some important details. One of the main things they miss, which is often a career killer, is that their boss may not share their priorities.

For many Inspirers, the caregivers in their family systems conditioned them to trust that authority figures will be genuinely interested in their ideas. This assumption can be overly optimistic when their boss is operating from another quadrant.

Watch for Clues That Your Boss Is Tuning You Out

Bear in mind that some superiors don't particularly care what you think or how you feel unless you outrank them. This is particularly true when the boss is a Commander. While the Inspirer might legitimately think his or her insights should be important to the boss, the Commander often doesn't care what people below them in the hierarchy think about anything. Remember, the Commander isn't really in love with the idea of brainstorming anyway. They'd much rather be storming the next hill. If they are going to force themselves to stop rushing around long enough to converse with anyone, odds are that they are only going to make this effort for someone who outranks them. However, it's not just Commanders who start glancing at their watches impatiently when the enthusiastic Inspirer gets wound up. Don't forget that your boss may have deadlines and priorities you know nothing about. Stay alert for body language, and exit gracefully when you are losing the attention of your boss.

Realize That Original Thinking Can Prompt an Organizational Backlash

If you work in a large firm where your boss isn't the CEO or founder, bear in mind that original thinking is not always met with appreciation. Whenever there's room for improvement in any organization, if the place is big enough, you can bet that somebody's siphoning power off for themselves at precisely the spot where things are breaking down. Because of their seniority, your boss may be able to assess the potential resistance to a new idea better than you can. Thus, regardless of how rational your argument for any improvement may be, brace yourself for the power plays you, and by extension your boss, may encounter if you end up stepping on someone else's turf—even when you are tiptoeing around for the greater good.

Be Careful Not to Upstage Your Boss!

Your boss may not telegraph how enraged he or she gets when someone yanks the spotlight away from them, but upstaging the boss is a risk that's just not worth taking. Your best bet is to share your most innovative ideas with your superior in such a way that they feel it will be to their advantage to share the credit with you. If you end up reporting to someone who establishes a pattern of grabbing credit for your work, then you may need to try to reposition your career so you can report to someone with more intellectual integrity. That said, rarely is any one idea worth potentially sabotaging your relationship with your superior. Inspirers who outshine their superiors at the wrong moment have received everything from mysteriously negative performance reviews to pink slips.

Don't Leave Prematurely—or Abruptly

One of the biggest challenges presents itself when the Inspirer decides that his or her boss is exhibiting behavior that clashes with the Inspirer's ethical code. This is because most Inspirers can't work for someone they don't respect for a protracted period of time. Many Inspirers have told me that having a boss who is focused on his or her personal advantage at the expense of the organization is something they can't tolerate for long. The Inspirer often feels compelled to get away from this type of boss because the emotional strain of trying to make sense of out of what the Inspirer perceives to be toxic behavior feels overwhelming. When this is the case, the Inspirer needs to remember that how they leave an organization is often as important as what they have accomplished there when it comes to their ongoing reputation. Regardless of how you feel about your boss, take the time to lay your transitional groundwork carefully. Remember, some bosses rarely think *they* have done anything wrong, because in their minds, it's always somebody else's fault. Thus, if you leave them in the lurch, they may find some creative ways to punish you.

Power Grid Case Study

Toni, a single mother of Native American descent, is an Inspirer who keeps the books and does most of the general management for a non-profit organization dedicated to helping women below the poverty line get the job skills they need to support their families. Bonnie is a Charmer who has recently left a high-profile job in the private sector to run this nonprofit. We met both of these women in chapter 5, when we explored the scenario from the perspective of the Charmer.

Toni was initially thrilled that Bonnie was going to be her boss. Bonnie looked like the type of confident career woman Toni had always admired.

Unfortunately, as time passed, Toni's admiration for Bonnie began to deteriorate. As an Inspirer, Toni valued using the resources of the organization to benefit the greater good and focused on helping the agency operate frugally. Toni's first red flag came when she started going over the bank statement and thought that the agency had been double charged for their monthly utilities. To her horror, Toni discovered that the huge extra debit was money Bonnie had withdrawn to take a popular journalist out to lunch! Until that day, Toni didn't even know it was possible to spend that much money on a single meal.

Raised to believe that people in authority would be interested in her concerns, Toni decided to discuss the budget dilemma with Bonnie. In many ways, this was a strong professional response. By dealing with a Charmer boss directly and diplomatically, Inspirers are often able to maintain their relationship with the boss and sustain their self-respect as the inevitable clash of values between these two types runs its course. In fact, in some situations, by not confronting a Charmer boss, the Inspirer may run the risk of coming across as a doormat.

While Bonnie was reassuring, Toni got the uncomfortable feeling that she was being "handled" rather than heard. A couple of weeks later, Toni discovered that one of Bonnie's lavish lunches had wiped out the funds the agency had earmarked to host a party to benefit unwed mothers. Toni responded by leaving Bonnie a polite letter of resignation.

Inspirers can't keep working for a boss whose values they don't respect. When they share their opinions with the boss, the Inspirer has to be careful not to become overly hopeful that such conversations will lead to behavioral change. The bottom line with these two is that since the Inspirer is focused on what benefits the system while Charmers are focused on what furthers their personal agenda, the clash of values between them takes place on so many levels that it's often only a matter of time before the Inspirer leaves.

As with many Inspirers, once Toni lost respect for her boss, she began to check out mentally before she actually resigned. Regardless of her personal feelings about Bonnie, Toni stopped operating by her own highest values when she stopped striving to find a way to communicate her convictions about what was best for the organization. Inspirers must remember that how and why they leave an organization is often as important to their professional reputations as the hard work they have done during their active tenure. Obviously, tactfully lining up an alternative job opportunity is important for the Inspirer's career momentum. However, it's equally important for the Inspirer to use such transitional moments as an opportunity to clearly voice their professional concerns for the sake of the remaining employees and clients of the organizations that have employed them.

Conclusion

While Inspirers' motives often have heroic undertones, the blind spot most Inspirers struggle with involves becoming so fixated on their vision of how things could be that they overlook details vital to grappling with circumstances as they are.

While some types on the grid have to work to tune in to their inner voice, the Inspirer's challenge is often the reverse. The volume on the Inspirer's "voice from within" is often so loud that it drowns out the potentially helpful input that colleagues from other types on the Power Grid can share with them.

Applying their creativity to the here and now starts to happen naturally once the Inspirer begins to embrace the resources in their business structure. By developing a more balanced power style, the Inspirer learns how to work with office politics rather than being worked over by them. They learn how to command the respect of their peers rather than becoming targets of envy. They also learn how to evolve from being well-intentioned mentors into being strong managers.

The more the Inspirer practices these skills, the better they get at maneuvering around restrictions rather than hanging up their jersey and leaving the field when they hit a bureaucratic hurdle. This, as we know, is the birth of political savvy.

CHAPTER TEN

Putting the Power Grid into Action

The premise of this chapter is simple: habits matter. When pressure heats up on the job, it's ambitious to assume you're going to think clearly. When emotions are running high around us and inside us, the majority of us begin operating on automatic pilot. The action plan in this chapter will help you use what you've learned throughout this book to upgrade the operating system that kicks in when your capacity for logic gets knocked out.

The good news is that reconditioning yourself to play to your strengths is simple. The challenging news is that it requires dedication. I mention the importance of dedication up front because as an executive coach, I've met many people who are eager for a quick fix. Today, many of us have been seduced into believing that if something doesn't work quickly, it doesn't work at all. The Power Grid is not a quick fix. It's taken you most of your life to develop the responses that dictate your power style. Some aspects of your power genes work in your favor, and some are blind spots that undermine your efforts. The destructive ones aren't going to disappear overnight without some active effort on your part.

My coaching experience over the last decade has taught me that engaging in the right sequence of self-reflective exercises and subsequent action steps is crucial for achieving sustainable professional growth. The sequence of steps outlined in this reconditioning process is designed to guide you through the work of learning and unlearning in tandem. Just as we inhale and exhale to keep moving forward in life, alternating periods of action and reflection keep us progressing in our careers. You can't just think yourself into a more powerful operating style; you need to experiment with new patterns of behavior and experience what goes on with your internal and external triggers to evolve effectively.

In my first book, *The Authentic Career,* I introduced clients to a four-stage process for evaluating their professional priorities that took them through an in-depth exploration of why they might have chosen their current career path.[1] Part of this process involves guidance on how to deal with the emotional backlash that often prevents us from considering a broader range of professional options. Think of this emotional backlash the way you would the choppy part of the surf that can impede your journey into the deeper and smoother part of the ocean. If you hang on and don't turn back, the best part of your journey is yet to come.

How Blind Spots Impede Positive Change

The emotional backlash that thwarts positive change echoes the way that our blind spots work on the Power Grid. When you are facing a professional challenge, your blind spots work to keep you operating on automatic pilot. They kick in to protect you from what you would prefer not to know about yourself. Unfortunately, these same blind spots simultaneously prevent you from considering the fullest range of potential responses when your power is threatened on the job.

Blind spots kick in when we lose perspective and the less effective aspects of our power genes shift us into automatic pilot so we can avoid uncomfortable feelings. Just as with a car that gets poor gas mileage, when we are driven by the need to deny certain aspects of our emotional reality, we simply aren't using our energy effectively. The blind spots that take over are all too predictable. The Pleaser wastes valuable time and energy trying to gain approval from people who either take their hard work for granted or, in a worst-case scenario, manipulate them and discard them when they burn out. The Charmer starts isolating, driven by the need to avoid his or her inner demons. The Commander can get crazy about winning at all costs. And the Inspirer can lapse into fantasy and overlook the details needed to make his or her concepts commercially viable.

Blind spots get lodged in our psyches because the brain is basically a pleasure-seeking organ. Thus, it's not surprising that most of the automatic responses we have developed kick in because our subconscious is hardwired to avoid things that make us uncomfortable. As we have seen, this wiring process begins in the family system, where we learned how to get what we wanted and needed from our early caregivers by observing and intuiting their reactions under pressure. When Pleasers could finally get their preoccupied parents to turn around and pay attention to them, their stress abated and they felt emotional relief. When Charmers were able to soothe a needy caregiver, they felt as if they could temporarily relax. When Commanders were rising in the pecking order, the accompanying surge of adrenaline (and relief) produced an emotional high. Finally, nothing brightens the day of an Inspirer like discovering a new solution to an old problem. The rush of pleasure the Inspirer feels echoes what they felt when they heard the applause of proud parents who encouraged their inventiveness.

You can bet that when your blind spots kick in, you are not consciously in control. As we have seen with all types on the grid, when you are feeling anxious or exhausted, you snap into automatic pilot and your awareness narrows. When that happens, your range of options can seem fairly slim. When clients call me to say that they had no choice but to storm out on their boss or blow off a demanding client, I know that the blind spot won that round. Reflecting on the Power Grid when you have a stretch of time on a long airplane flight is one thing. However, putting the Power Grid into practice when your colleague is trying to undermine you for a key promotion is, as we say in Texas, a horse of a different color. That's the horse to bet on.

The Reconditioning Process

This process is designed to help you recognize the instinctual reflexes you have developed that have worked in your favor professionally—based on how you have been conditioned in your family system. The objective is to identify the natural strengths inherent in your power genes so you can play to them more effectively.

A second, and complementary, goal is to clarify where your blind spots have been systematically diminishing your professional potential. As these self-sabotaging reactions are identified, you are going to learn how to recondition yourself so that when you get triggered, you are able to practice new and improved responses.

Cycling through the four stages of the reconditioning process will help you develop a deeper dialogue with yourself around power. In doing so, identifying the precise quadrant you resonate with most strongly is not as important as cultivating the ability to ask yourself more thought-provoking questions when you suspect you are being swept away by your blind spots and caught in the undertow of a power struggle on the job.

Excerpts from the case study of Larry, the Pleaser mentioned in the first chapter, will be used to illustrate each of the stages of the reconditioning process. You may recall that Larry was the first head of corporate communications to be considered for partner at his investment firm. As a result, Larry's power style was being evaluated by the top brass at his firm. Reviewing Larry's reconditioning work, stage by stage, will give you a personal glimpse of how one client used the Power Grid to create an action plan to keep his promotion on track when his encounters with senior managers took him out of his comfort zone.

The Four Stages of the Reconditioning Process

1. Identify Your Power Quadrant(s)—A Self-Reflection Stage

In any change process, the first thing you want to do is identify your strengths and your starting point. This initial stage is where you begin a deeper dialogue with yourself by clarifying the quadrant or quadrants that you identify with most strongly. You are engaged in this part of the process right now, and some part of your mind has been testing the waters of self-reflection as you have been reading through this book.

This first stage is built on a simple truth: you can't improve what you don't understand. As you increase your awareness of how the balance of power in your family system has forged your habitual responses to authority on the job and shaped your power genes, you will be able to appreciate the ways that your innate strengths and your recurrent challenges influence emotions and behavior.

If you have difficulty pinpointing the quadrants you operate from most frequently, it's helpful to take the time to think of one person you are close to personally (such as your spouse or best friend) and one person who you've worked with in an ongoing professional context. With these two individuals in mind, write out the four to five strengths and blind spots you suspect each person would use to describe you. Then, take this list of qualities and consider the quadrant that you think is most reflective of these traits. If, in your opinion, some qualities assigned to you fall into more than one quadrant, feel free to list every quadrant where you think these characteristics might belong. Then, simply count. The quadrants that come up most frequently are a good starting place in terms of graphing yourself on the Power Grid.

Stage 1 Case Study

After his initial review of the Power Grid, Larry felt that he operated as both a Pleaser and an Inspirer. While he suspected that he was grappling with a Pleaser blind spot as he struggled to impress members of senior management, he was also convinced that much of his career advancement stemmed from his ability to draw on the strengths of an Inspirer.

Larry's initial self-assessment was fair enough. After all, as we now know, there are no right or wrong answers to the questions on the Power Grid. The central purpose of this framework is to help people develop a deeper dialogue with themselves around how they deal with power in the workplace and why. What's more, many people find that their strengths are clustered in one quadrant, while the predominant blind spots they grapple with stem from a different quadrant on the grid.

Taking a closer look at Larry's family system clarifies how and why this happens. Larry's mother and father shared a deep respect for each other, and while they were both committed to a spiritual approach to life, his mother was a devout Catholic but his father never embraced a particular religion. Their shared commitment to ethical living, as well as their tolerance of each other's viewpoints, made a case for this family system being one that might easily foster an Inspirer.

However, when Larry took the time to examine some of the more emotionally charged memories from his childhood, it was clear that he didn't get the attention and validation he longed for from his parents. A highly creative student, Larry was often crushed when his parents barely had time to acknowledge his latest accomplishment because they were preoccupied with the drama surrounding his alcoholic brother. To keep his parents from feeling even guiltier about a situation they couldn't control, Larry suppressed his feelings by working even harder. These feelings rarely bubbled up to the surface unless Larry found himself in one of those situations where he was on the verge of getting the type of attention he had craved for so long. Larry's need to impress members of his senior management team tapped directly into this Pleaser blind spot.

As Larry's situation illustrates, no family system will be fully aligned with any one power style. Even in the most rigid Commander families, there are going to be moments when the parents work as an even-handed team and perhaps even choose to bend the rules when dealing with their kids. What the Power Grid gives you is a framework for understanding the emotional and behavior patterns that characterized your family system the highest percentage of the time. As you consider these percentages, bear in mind that your emotional memory of the dynamics that took place between you and your parents is a far more powerful force than any third party's objective assessment of the facts.

Considering how his wife and one of his closest colleagues would describe him helped Larry clarify the quadrants he needed to focus on to operate more effectively.

In Larry's case, he felt his wife would list his strengths as:

1. Loyalty

2. Good networking skills

3. Empathy for others

4. Strong work ethic

In contrast, Larry felt one of his key staff members, Jason, would describe his strengths as:

1. Successful in delivering results

2. Team player

3. Good at expressing appreciation

4. High energy and charismatic

Larry then went on to group the strengths he felt his wife and Jason would use to describe him into the power styles he decided they represented on the Power Grid as follows:

1. Loyalty—Pleaser

2. Good networking skills—Charmer/Inspirer

3. Empathy for others—Pleaser

4. Strong work ethic—Pleaser

5. Successful in delivering results—Commander

6. Team player—Pleaser/Inspirer

7. Good at expressing appreciation—Pleaser

8. High energy and charismatic—Inspirer

Thus, when it came to his strengths, Larry realized that he put five of the characteristics he thought others would use to describe him in the Pleaser category. Larry also had one strength he considered descriptive of the Charmer power style, one that represented the Commander, and three that he listed in the Inspirer category. The bottom line? Larry discovered that many of the strengths others might use to describe him were representative of the Pleaser and Inspirer power styles.

Larry went on to do a similar grouping of the blind spots he felt others would use to describe him. Nearly all the blind spots Larry thought people close to him might use to describe him fell in the Pleaser category. This simple exercise helped Larry realize that when it came to some of the less effective reflexes he needed to correct to get ahead, overcoming blind spots associated with Pleasers was an area where he needed to start focusing.

Many clients I have worked with find that working through the first stage of the reconditioning process can be a self-reflection tool in itself. Pleasers tend to think carefully about how others are likely to describe them, and strive to "get it right." Charmers breeze through this exercise quickly to avoid getting emotionally engaged. Commanders critique everything from the number of comments to the objectivity of the people that come to mind for them, searching for flaws every step of the way. Inspirers are often tempted to focus on finding new ways to use this feedback process, and need to be mindful of staying in the moment and applying their answers to themselves and their current challenges.

2. Learn to Take Strategic Pauses—An Action Stage

Once you have given yourself credit for the strengths inherent in the quadrant(s) you habitually operate from, it's time to start to deal with the blind spots that may have accumulated over time. This second stage of the reconditioning process begins as your heightened awareness of your power genes enhances your ability to choose the way you will respond to challenging situations rather than slipping into automatic pilot. For most clients, the second stage begins after they have had a couple of weeks to reflect on the power quadrants they identify with most strongly. As you go about your job, you will find the second stage kicking in when situations that used to drive you to automatically lose your temper, sneak out for a cigarette, or fantasize about calling a headhunter begin to strike you as learning opportunities rather than potential threats.

An important parallel exists between operating powerfully on the job and driving a car: being able to stop can save the day. Developing the "inner brakes" necessary to pause when you are triggered and about to lapse into a blind spot requires both commitment and courage. The two seconds that it takes to suspend an automatic reaction when you feel that your power base is threatened can feel like the longest two seconds of your life. Remember, you are never responsible for your first thought. Your first thought may run something like, How dare he meet with my client without taking me along . . . I'll make him pay!

This type of defensive thinking can shoot through your brain like a meteor racing through the night sky. What you are responsible for is noticing this first thought and then taking control of your second thought. Practicing the inner action of taking a strategic pause between your first thought (a conditioned response) and your second thought (a choice) builds the foundation of inner discipline necessary to stop reacting and start responding more powerfully under pressure.

Stage 2 Case Study

Having determined that gaining a solid understanding of both the Inspirer and the Pleaser power genes was important for him, Larry proceeded to start tackling his most troublesome blind spots. To do this, he had to become particularly conscious of the emotional and physiological triggers that kicked in when he was most tempted to indulge in self-sabotaging behavior. This is a simple concept but a challenging task.

By strengthening his understanding of his own automatic actions and reactions, Larry found that he was able to better withstand the tension that took place inside him when one of the senior partners he was trying to bond with seemed disinterested during a casual conversation with him.

One morning, when he was seated between two senior partners at a firm off-site, Larry sat in agonized silence while the two of them began chatting avidly about their golf games—acting as if he were invisible. He was dying to find a way to join this conversation. His emotional trigger around wanting to be noticed was causing him to feel like an anxious second grader—and to squirm in his seat like one.

At that moment, Larry remembered to take a strategic pause and pay attention to what was happening to him on the inside. He realized that his first thought was that he needed to improve his golf game so he could "fit in" better.

Rather than saying anything in haste, Larry began to wonder how a confident person who didn't care how these guys reacted to him might respond in this situation. In a flash, Larry had a realization that shifted his emotional energy as well as the energy of the moment surrounding him. It dawned on him that a confident person wouldn't feel the need to do anything. They wouldn't force a change of subject, and they wouldn't try to force their way into a conversation they knew little about. A confident person would simply be in the moment and enjoy a second cup of coffee. As Larry's perspective brightened, the partners surrounding him suddenly seemed to notice his presence, and the conversation shifted naturally to a topic he could enjoy. Larry hadn't changed anything but his attitude.

Remember, your ability to stop reacting ineffectively and start responding more powerfully begins with your *second thought*. Under emotional pressure, your first thought is often a conditioned response that cycles through your brain like a loop in a computer program. It's your second thought that represents your ability to objectively assess your own power reflexes and take the strategic pause necessary stop recycling bad habits and start practicing new ones.

As you develop the new habit of taking a strategic pause when you get triggered, your sense of perspective returns. Your inner world gets bigger than your blind spot as you gain perspective and the capacity to make more powerful choices is restored.

3. Reflect on Your Power Patterns and Their Hidden Costs—A Self-Reflection Stage

For most clients, it takes at least a month before they are ready to engage in the third stage of the reconditioning process. This is because many people find they have to experience the benefits of playing to their strengths more consistently before they develop the inner courage necessary to face what their blind spots have cost them emotionally and financially.

Watching someone in the early days of the reconditioning process hold their tongue when they are *dying* to give "some idiot" a piece of their mind can feel like watching a volcano decide not to explode. There's a lot of pent up energy here, and it's going to have to be channeled somewhere. The most constructive place to channel this energy is into self-reflection. Many clients report that as they struggle to slow down their behavior on the outside, their thoughts speed up on the inside as their mind tries to pressure them into indulging in their same old habits.

"Give him a piece of your mind; you'll feel better," the mind in search of emotional relief urges. "Walk out of here now; you are better than this!" prompts the irate voice of the psyche. It's at this crucial moment that you want to reflect on the voices in your head rather than blindly obeying them. Whose voice is this anyway? Is it yours? Your father's? Your spouse's?

As you start learning to reflect rather than react, you will become increasingly aware of how your power genes play out on the job by noticing the following:

- It's not just the source of the messages but the messages themselves that bear scrutiny at these moments. Where has this behavior gotten you in the past? What might be driving the other person's reaction to you? The better you get at taking strategic pauses when you are triggered, the more your sense of perspective gets restored.

- As you recondition yourself to take a few precious seconds to reflect before you react, you will begin to notice the previously hidden costs of running away from your feelings by going into automatic pilot. Have you been spending money you couldn't afford to medicate the frustration you feel over placating people you resent? Have you made risky investment decisions because you didn't have the courage you needed to take meaningful risks to advance your career? Did you accept a job that promised a career track they couldn't deliver on because you were too

impatient to do your homework on the organization before you joined? Do you buy lottery tickets hoping you will win millions and all these tough questions will just disappear? Assessing these hidden costs is not intended to discourage you. It's intended to reinforce your commitment to working through your blind spots so you can operate more powerfully in all facets of your career.

- When the hidden costs of denying your blind spots compound over time and the emotional bill comes due, you may experience a power turning point. Such turning points enable you to come to terms with ways that you have inadvertently given your power away at such a deep level that you become able to readjust more than your conscious attitude. This type of deeper realization empowers you to begin to rework your less conscious (and more emotional) reactions to workplace triggers.

Stage 3 Case Study

By stopping himself from anxiously babbling in stage 2, Larry had actively taken control of his internal emotions and reacted in a positive way outwardly. During the precious seconds it took for him to overcome his mind's urgent command to fill the silence by verbally "tap dancing" for the other men at his table, Larry had unleashed a hornet's nest of anxious voices on the inside. Meanwhile, on the outside, Larry needed to behave calmly until his trigger subsided.

As Larry learned over time to channel the pent-up energy he was managing on the inside away from self-sabotage and toward self-reflection, he made some important discoveries about himself.

The more he practiced holding his tongue when he felt insecure, the more Larry began to realize that the lack of confidence he felt around members of senior management had made him into a workaholic. The problem was that while he was working hard, he wasn't working

smart. Driven by the belief that he could "never do enough" to prove his worth, Larry agonized over the details and missed the big picture when it came to important initiatives. One of the biggest areas where he lost track of the big picture was with regard to his own net worth.

Larry was so focused on helping the members of senior management explain their financial strategy to the media that he forgot to look out for his own finances. As he burned the midnight oil, Larry failed to keep a watchful eye on the investments in his retirement account. What's worse, because he felt guilty for spending so much time at the office, he turned a blind eye while his teenage son ran up credit card charges that put his first year of college tuition at risk. This financial hardship was even causing some strain to his marriage.

Larry experienced a power turning point the night he made the realization that he had been emotionally abandoning his son the way his own father had abandoned him. Like overlapping weather patterns that can take on the force of a thunderstorm, power turning points take place when our psyches are snapped out of their normal operating pattern of "underawareness." The walls of denial we have constructed to protect our blind spots begin to crumble when the emotional charge of memories we have been suppressing from the past begins to mix with new realizations about our present. Larry's power turning point caused him to go back to the Power Grid and take a harder look at the blind spots associated with the Pleaser. After doing this, Larry resolved to make some important changes so he could operate more effectively on the job and in his life.

The hidden costs of your blind spots can provide clues to the power quadrants you operate from when you are under pressure. As we have seen, the Pleaser who hasn't developed strong self-promotional skills often pays the high price of not being given full credit for his or her efforts and getting passed over for promotions. Charmers, who are highly image conscious, may accumulate financial debt through lavish spending on clothing, entertaining, or even vacations, to "take the edge off" when pressure mounts on the job. Commanders, whose tendency

to be gruff and impatient can sometimes take root in the home as well as on the job, may become emotionally estranged from loved ones. Finally, when Inspirers don't keep their feet on the ground, they often pay the price of watching more organized competitors reap the benefits of some of their best thinking.

What are some of the hidden costs you are facing in life? Are you underemployed? Overleveraged? Emotionally isolated? By considering some of the key challenges you are facing in your life today, you may be able to clarify the blind spots that have caused these various types of costs to accumulate. By becoming aware of the price you pay for your blind spots, you enhance your resolve to replace less effective habits with new ways of responding to old challenges.

4. Practice New Habits—An Action Stage

If we are designed to mentally go into automatic pilot under stress, then we want to upgrade our internal operating system so that the habits that kick in when our brain shuts down work for us rather than against us. Reinforcing the positive habits that are foundational to this inner upgrade is what this final stage of the reconditioning process is all about. Most clients start the fourth stage of the reconditioning process within two to three months of being introduced to the Power Grid. This stage evolves naturally as you discover new solutions to old problems on the job. The more mindful you become of the ways your power genes influence the tone you set professionally, the more the habit of playing to your natural strengths shifts from becoming something you focus on consciously to something you are conditioning yourself to do automatically.

This final stage of the process is where you squarely face the challenge of unlearning the habits that may undermine your professional advancement. As you tackle this, it's important to remember that new habits are easier to adopt than old ones are to eliminate. This is because we only have our conscious mind to contend with when we are trying to practice something new. We can read a book, solicit advice from a trusted friend, or even find something inspirational in a film, and get plenty of ideas for new and empowering career strategies. All you have to do to put a new strategy into practice is make a conscious commitment to give the new behavior a fair try.

However, old habits can maintain a firm grip on our psyches. It often takes releasing the emotional energy that is fueling our habitual responses to unwind an old behavior, and that can take longer—sometimes years. This is because reconditioning an old habit that's become part of your unconscious operating system requires ongoing work. This is also why, as much as we long for them, quick fixes can't produce lasting change. Sustainable change requires us to do more than think differently. To achieve sustainable change, we must consistently practice new habits in response to old triggers.

Stage 4 Case Study

Consistently learning to pause before speaking, and speaking succinctly and deliberately, became a life preserver for Larry. So much so, in fact, that he developed a reputation among the senior partners for being a man of few words—but a man of important words.

Since the core blind spots he was reworking came from the Pleaser quadrant, Larry worked to consciously enhance the Pleaser's strengths that came to him naturally as he worked through his reconditioning process. Pleasers innately realize that many people prefer to hear themselves talk than to listen. By keeping this in mind, Larry developed the habit of listening intently to those around him. As this new skill became second nature to him, Larry branched out and studied the Charmer quadrant to learn more techniques for successfully engaging the members of senior management who were now seeking him out in the hallways. Considering the role of seduction in relationship building inspired Larry to begin to listen to comedy tapes in his car to brush up on jokes that would help him lighten tense moments, and maintain eye contact to convey a sense of confidence. Within a month of starting his campaign to convey a more confident tone on the job, Larry was given the promotion he longed for.

After he had made partner, the real work started for Larry. Now that the beauty pageant was over, the stakes were higher and the gloves were off. Larry found himself engaged in ongoing power plays with experienced Charmers and Commanders who were willing to do much more than withdraw their approval; they were willing to engage in all-out warfare to get what they wanted. Larry found himself cycling through the stages of the reconditioning process repeatedly as he won some power plays and lost some others. He began to gain the respect of his colleagues, and to respect himself, as he learned to draw on a more agile power style that incorporated a balance of strengths from all four quadrants. One of the strengths he drew on the most, which tapped into the Inspirer dimension of his family system, was a healthy sense of humor about the ongoing challenges facing members of senior management. As Larry developed more internal balance in the way that he responded emotionally and behaviorally on the job, he found he was also enjoying more external balance as well. Larry gradually developed the self-confidence he needed to shift his mental focus away from work at the end of the day so he could be present for his family as well as his firm.

One of the main benefits of the Power Grid is that it clarifies the ways we can all play to our strengths. By listing how others close to him would describe his strengths, Larry was able to see ways that he exhibited positive power reflexes from both the Pleaser and the Inspirer quadrants. In my experience, people who fail to give themselves sufficient credit for their strengths sabotage their careers just as fast as people who ignore their blind spots. Using the Power Grid will help you draw on your existing strengths with confidence as you begin the work of replacing self-sabotaging reactions with more effective professional habits.

Power Patterns in the Headlines

Life is not an accidental experience. Everything from our first love to our last overdue bill notice presents us with lessons about power. As we've seen, stories are powerful learning tools. Reflecting on the Power Grid as you consider the headlines describing leaders who are amassing (or losing) power is an exercise that can deepen your own understanding of power on the job.

Every day we are blasted with news that recounts the exploits of business leaders, politicians, and entertainers who have done something that captures the public's imagination and makes many of us say to ourselves some variation of "Thank God that wasn't me!" I've had clients from around the world draw on their assessment of the power styles of public figures ranging from Eliot Spitzer to Albert Einstein to deepen their own understanding of the way a leader's power genes can influence their legacy in politics, business, and even scientific research. As they do this, clients become more and more aware that there's always an explanation for why people do what they do—especially when it comes to power. The key is that the explanation may not be found purely by examining the mind of the individual. It may also have its roots in the way this person has been conditioned by the systems that have shaped his or her life's journey.

What's Your Power Turning Point?

As you work through the four stages of the reconditioning process, like Larry from our case study, you are likely to run into a power turning point of your own. This can be either a public or private moment in your own life when your growing awareness of how your power genes have influenced your operating style snaps you out of automatic pilot. Clients who have experienced power turning points report confronting some challenging questions when the part of their mind that has learned to shut down in the face of strong emotions comes back online. Why am I responding this way? Is there something I need to know about this situation I'm unaware of? How does the person I'm working with feel about themselves in this moment? Power turning points take place when you have developed a strong enough relationship with yourself to ask deeper questions about habitual reactions you had previously taken for granted. This enhanced capacity for self-reflection is the cornerstone of personal and professional growth.

Here's some good news: it takes less energy to learn to operate more powerfully than it does to stay stuck. Here's some even better news: working with your power genes can be fun and self-perpetuating because the person who was conditioned to give his or her power away was a child. The person focused on reworking these patterns is an adult.

Wielding Your Personal Power

Honesty is a luxury owned by the powerful. Anyone who has ever watched a small child cower before an irritated parent or heard a junior employee tell a white lie to keep a demanding superior from getting testy realizes this. When you obscure your true intentions and your ability to be truthful feels compromised, it's because you've sprung a power leak on some level.

As you continue to cycle through the four stages of the reconditioning process, you gradually cultivate the strength to own the truth about how your dormant and dominant power genes reflect your relationships with yourself. Whenever you experience a professional challenge, for example, whether it's being overlooked because you don't effectively promote yourself or it's self-sabotage because you aren't managing your stress, this theme reflects an imbalance of power within yourself. What we do is important, but asking the deeper question of why we are doing it is the gateway to gaining power in the future.

Over the years, I've taken some heat for asking people to take a deeper look at power patterns they'd prefer to ignore. People's minds often engage in elaborate gymnastics to keep them in their comfort zones. An example that comes to mind is a presentation our team did for a prominent women's networking organization. While most of the room was buzzing with positive energy, I spent the lunch break reassuring a hedge fund manager of Asian American descent that she could risk examining the link between her operating style as a leader and the way she had been conditioned to respond to her father. As we took some one-on-one time to explore the various ways that people reconciled their respect for authority figures with their right to question authority across cultures, she was able to realize that this work isn't about blame; it's about freedom.

Years later, I'm still getting e-mails from this successful investor about how understanding her power genes has helped her become a more thoughtful mentor, mother, and even daughter. A self-identified Commander, she shared with me a letter she decided to write to her deceased father. During his life, this man had ruled their family and their family business with an iron fist. In this letter, she praised what his power had accomplished in the international business community. Clarity starts with honesty, and she knew she had to be fair in her assessment of the strengths she had internalized from growing up in her father's orbit before she could explore the habits she wanted to rework. She then went on write her own "declaration of independence" from the blind spots that had forced her to operate with such a perpetual sense of urgency that she had shut off her access to her women's intuition. She explained that while she had learned to think fast under pressure, the sheer speed of her thoughts often sent her crashing into her blind spot. For years, she had impatiently terminated promising employees when their learning curve wasn't fast enough for her. This hurt her business as many of her former research analysts went to work for her competitors. She also found that she was unable to stop obsessing about her work on the weekends, which was causing stress in her marriage. Through developing an awareness of how her power genes influenced her operating style on the job, she was able to gradually develop a more flexible approach to wielding power. As she did this, she stopped seeing herself through her father's eyes and started tapping into her own feelings. She reported that the more she was able to do this, the more her pattern of oppressively controlling others was beginning to abate. By continuing this work, she told me that her goal was to ease into a more balanced flow between her work and her life.

We Teach What We Need to Learn

This woman's breakthrough stuck with me because it brought me back to one of my own power turning points. As you will recall, a power turning point is one of those moments where a deeper understanding of what has shaped your power genes in past reactions helps snap you out of automatic pilot in the present.

In the late 1990s, I had received two Lipper Awards for having the top-performing short-term global income fund in the United States. Fueled by a nonstop rush of adrenaline and caffeine, I was working day and night. I was on the trading floor by 5:30 most mornings, and I didn't head home until well after dark. We were running one of the first mutual funds in America to use derivatives as part of its currency hedging strategy, and my work was my mission.

One morning, as I was nervously pacing behind the traders, one of our brightest new research analysts tapped me on the shoulder and said politely, "Maggie, do you have a minute?"

Jumpy from way too many cups of coffee, I barked back at him, "If it isn't going to make money for us in the next fifteen minutes, I don't have the time!" Suddenly, silence descended across our part of the trading floor. Anyone who has ever been on a trading floor knows that silence is a rare occurrence, and when it does happen, it feels a little ominous.

A couple of the traders looked over their shoulders nervously and then hurriedly returned to their screens. I turned to face the analyst I'd just publicly slimed. His face was red, and he was fighting back the emotions welling up inside him. I felt mortified. As I started to apologize, he turned on his heel and raced off the floor so no one else could see that he was justifiably hurt. Much like the Ultimate Fighting Championship (UFC) Octagon, the trading floor wasn't the place for feelings in those days.

I tried apologizing, and he tried accepting, but the emotional damage was done. He left our firm six months later and went on to become a well-respected portfolio manager at another organization.

As I tried to come to terms with what had happened that morning, I asked myself, What were you thinking! Guess what I realized? I wasn't thinking. My mind was running on fear, and brains that run on fear don't think—they recycle. The only thing happening above my neck that morning was an endless litany of What if this goes wrong? What if that goes wrong? I wasn't aware of anyone else around me that morning, which was why I popped off like a jerk. Computers may be more powerful when they work faster, but that's not always the case with the human mind. Often, to operate more powerfully, we have to know when to slow down as well as when to speed up.

While this power turning point on the trading floor felt like a career "speed bump" at the time, it taught me numerous lessons about power. One that I hope adds value for you when it comes to understanding our power genes is that what we do under pressure often isn't as important as why we do it. To the outside observer, and to several of the traders on that morning, I probably appeared to be reacting like a Commander who needed to switch to decaf. However, people who know me well realize that this incident isn't reflective of my dominant power style. I'm a Pleaser, and on that morning, I was a Pleaser who snapped.

Sometimes a Pleaser will bark like a Commander, and sometimes Commanders roll over and play dead when the people around them don't expect them to. The key to understanding your power genes comes from grasping how your emotional history plays into your spontaneous reactions. That morning, I was concerned that my investors, my bosses, and everyone else on the planet would withdraw their approval and decide I simply didn't have the "right stuff" to run that fund. My outburst wasn't driven by the sense of entitlement we associate with a Commander; it was driven by insecurity. Frankly, if I had been a Commander, I might not have shocked myself and everyone around me by breaking my pattern of being easily approachable.

As you work with the Power Grid, you will learn that it's important not to make snap judgments about others or about yourself. You can evaluate your power style simply by identifying your dominant behavioral patterns. However, to improve your power patterns, you have to dig deeper to get at the roots of why you systematically operate a certain way under pressure and how this understanding can inform constructive change.

Power Is Contagious

One thing the Power Grid teaches us all is that when you undermine yourself, people around you suffer. As children, we often didn't have the luxury of choice when dealing with our caregivers. Many of us felt compelled to bury uncomfortable feelings, to please, placate, or even protect the authority figures who raised us. Obediently, many of us suppressed our messier emotions—even from ourselves. The problem is, when we bury uncomfortable feelings, we bury our power of choice right along with them. From that initial moment, we start to establish the power patterns we need to survive emotionally in the first system we have ever known. And we carry these patterns and behaviors with us into adulthood.

As adults, when we are anxious or exhausted, we often feel just as cornered and desperate as we did when we were little kids. This is when automatic pilot takes over. Whether it's a Pleaser placating a bully or a Commander acting like one, when any of us fall into the grip of our blind spots we often trigger similarly unconscious patterns from those around us.

Fortunately, the process of consciously learning to play to the strengths inherent in your power genes also has a ripple effect. By taking a few seconds to reflect on our first thought before our reactions kick in, we give those around us the room they need to do the same thing. What's more, as we learn to set a more powerful tone with those around us, we gain the respect of someone far more important than our top clients or even our latest boss. We gain respect for ourselves. If there's one opinion you want to learn to respect under pressure on the job, it's your own.

A Deeper Dialogue Around Power

What's brought you to your current point in your professional journey, and where do you go from here? As you reflect on how your power genes have shaped your professional legacy thus far, it's important to consider how developing a fuller understanding of your personal history can strengthen your most important business relationship. That, of course, is your relationship with yourself.

Having had the unique opportunity to listen to the personal hopes, dreams, and challenges of people from all levels of the professional spectrum, I've had the good fortune to witness many variations on a consistent theme: when you stop trusting yourself, you start losing power. "I *knew* that was a bad idea, but I did it anyway because . . ." is a common refrain from people who have experienced a power setback. Being able to have a deeper dialogue with others about power can make you a compelling conversationalist. However, being able to have a deeper dialogue with *yourself* about power can help you chart your own professional destiny rather than waiting for someone else to call the shots for you.

Your career is one of your most prized possessions. As you become increasingly aware of how your power genes influence your operating style on the job, it's also one of your greatest gifts to others. As you develop a deeper dialogue with yourself around power, your professional tone will begin to empower everyone around you. When we tap into the power that comes from inner acceptance, in a myriad of verbal and nonverbal ways we give those around us the room they need to operate more powerfully as well.

My work with clients around the world has taught me that your power genes shape your behavior, and, over time, your behavior sculpts your overall character on the job and off. My hope is that the Power Grid will help you continue to ask yourself the questions that will empower you to lead with courage, collaborate with clarity, and fortify the self-confidence you need to realize your dreams.

NOTES

Chapter One

1. Maggie Craddock, *The Authentic Career: Following the Path of Self-Discovery to Professional Fulfillment* (Novato, CA: New World Library, 2004).

2. Salvador Minuchin, *Families and Family Therapy* (Cambridge, MA: Harvard University Press, 1974).

Chapter Two

1. Elie Wiesel, *Memoirs: All Rivers Run to the Sea* (New York: Alfred A. Knopf, 1995).

2. Cynthia Cooper, *Extraordinary Circumstances: The Journeys of a Corporate Whistleblower* (New Jersey: John Wiley & Sons, 2008).

3. Ibid., 23–24.

4. From Marion Woodman's talk at the second annual conference on Spirituality and Psychotherapy sponsored by the National Institute for the Psychotherapies in New York, April 30–May 2, 1999. See also Marion Woodman, *Addiction to Perfection: The Still Unravished Bride* (Toronto: Inner City Books, 1982).

Chapter Four

1. Darryl Strawberry with John Strausbaugh, *Straw: Finding My Way* (New York: Ecco, 2009), 77.

2. Jon Wiener, "Frank Sinatra: His Way," *The Nation*, June 15, 2009; http://www.thenation.com/article/frank-sinatra-his-way.

3. Stephen Koepp, Bill Johnson, and Frederick Ungeheur, "Money Was the Only Way," *Time*, December 1, 1986.

4. Amy Baker, *Adult Children of Parental Alienation Syndrome: Breaking the Ties That Bind* (New York: W. W. Norton & Company, 2007), 244.

Chapter Six

1. Jack Welch, *Jack: Straight from the Gut* (New York: Warner Business Books, 2001).

2. Norman Schwarzkopf, *It Doesn't Take a Hero* (New York: Bantam Books, 1993), 83.

3. Welch, *Jack*, 3.

4. Ibid., 3–4.

5. Ian D. Boardley and Maria Kavussanu, "Development and Validation of the Moral Disengagement in Sport Scale," *Journal of Sport and Exercise Psychology* 29 (2007): 608–628.

Chapter Eight

1. Jimmy Carter, *The Virtues of Aging* (New York: The Ballantine Publishing Group, 1988), 36.

2. Anthony Wolf, *Get Out of My Life, But First Could You Drive Me and Cheryl to the Mall?* (New York: The Noonday Press, 1991), 5.

3. Ibid., 6–7.

Chapter Ten

1. Maggie Craddock, *The Authentic Career: Following the Path of Self-Discovery to Professional Fulfillment* (Novato, CA: New World Library, 2004).

INDEX

accountability, 29, 94–96
achievement
   Commanders and, 112–113
   Pleasers and, 39
Ackerman, Nathan, 4
adaptability, 105, 116
Adult Children of Parental Alienation Syndrome (Baker), 74
aggression, Pleasers and, 53–57. *See also* conflict
all-or-nothing thinking, 106
All Rivers Run to the Sea (Wiesel), 26
altruism
   in Inspirers, 136, 138–139
   in Pleasers, 37–38
Angelou, Maya, 98
anxiety, in Pleasers, 33–34, 37, 48
Apple, 143
approval seeking, 6
   Charmers and, 73, 85
   by Pleasers, 11–12, 33–34, 37–39, 48, 49–50
assertiveness, of Pleasers, 32–33
AT&T, 143
attention seeking, 20–21
attitude, 182–183
The Authentic Career (Craddock), 3, 10, 174
authority
   Charmers and, 66–68, 73–75, 94, 97–98
   childhood responses to, 3–4
   Commanders and, 102–103, 130–133

Inspirers and, 137–138, 145–146
parents and, 5
Pleasers with, 48–53

backlash
   emotional, 174
   organizational, 167–168
Baker, Amy, 74
balance, 6
   for Inspirers, 144
   Inspirers and, 171
Bateson, Gregory, 4
behavioral styles, Power Grid, 9–11
Bertalanffy, Ludwig von, 4
Boesky, Ivan, 63, 68–69
bosses
   Charmers as, 84–89
   Commanders as, 104, 119, 120–125
   Inspirers as, 142–143, 158–162
   Inspirer subordinates and, 166–170
   Pleasers as, 48–53
   Pleaser subordinates and, 57–61
   upstaging, 168
brainstorming, 121, 167
Branson, Richard, 135
bureaucracy, 142–143
burnout, 144

Campbell, Joseph, 135
career tracks, 15–16, 198–199. *See also* transitions
   case studies on, 18–19
   of Charmers, 75–77

Index

career tracks (*continued*)
  of Commanders, 102, 129
  of Inspirers, 148–150, 168–169
  of Pleasers, 26, 31–32, 38–41, 47–48
Carter, Jimmy, 13, 138, 141
change
  blind spots as impediments to,
    174–176
  Charmers as agents of, 66–68, 81, 89
  Inspirers and, 158
  quick fixes and, 188–189
charisma, 136–137
Charmers, 12, 63–99
  blind spots of, 68–73, 175, 186
  as bosses, 84–89
  case studies on, 77–81, 86–89, 92–94,
    96–98
  as change agents, 66–68
  Commanders and, 127–129
  emotions as weakness and, 49, 71–73
  family background of, 73–75
  hidden agendas of, 86–87
  influence of, 64–65
  Inspirers and, 136, 152–154, 162
  in interviews, 41, 76–77
  isolation of, 71, 73, 85, 86–89
  manipulation by, 83
  as negotiators, 30
  as peers, 89–94
  Pleasers as bosses of, 50–53
  prevalence of, 63–64
  problem solving by, 66
  results by, 65–66, 68–69, 83–84
  self-reflection by, 109
  strengths of, 64–68
  as subordinates, 94–98
  transitions and, 41, 75–77
  work ethic of, 69–71
childhood. *See* family systems
Churchill, Winston, 119
collaboration
  Charmers and, 92–94
  Commanders and, 115–116, 125

comfort zones, 193–194
Commanders, 12–13, 101–134
  adaptability of, 105
  authority and, 67
  blind spots of, 106–110, 175, 186–187
  Charmer peers of, 91, 92–94
  emotions as weakness and, 49
  family system of, 39
  impatience of, 108–109
  Inspirer bosses of, 161–162
  Inspirers and, 162, 167
  Inspirers compared with, 139–140,
    146
  intolerance and insensitivity in,
    107–108
  leadership by, 104
  Pleaser subordinates and, 59–61
  prevalence of, 101
  resilience of, 104–105
  self-confidence of, 105–106
  strengths of, 102–106
  system versus individuals and,
    106–107
  in transitions, 41
  tunnel vision in, 109–110, 115–116
commitment
  to managing power, 2
  to reconditioning, 173
communication. *See also* interaction styles
  Commanders and, 107–109, 116–117,
    120–121, 161–162
  Inspirers and, 139–140, 154, 161–162
  with Pleasers, 57–59
  strategic pauses, 181–183
competition
  Charmers and, 89–90
  Commanders and, 113, 125–126
  Inspirers and, 162–163
conflict
  avoidance of, 31–33, 48–49
  Charmers and, 66–68, 89–90
  Commanders and, 121, 130, 131–133
  Inspirers and, 149

Pleasers and, 29–33, 48–50, 55, 58
resolution of, 29–31, 149
with self, 6–7
conformity, 14, 146
confrontation
Charmers and, 91 (*see also* conflict)
consensus seeking, 8
control
blind spots and, 174–176
Charmers and, 78
Commanders and, 13, 106
Cooper, Cynthia, 11, 25–26, 27–28, 29, 34
corruption, Pleasers and, 25–26, 27–28. *See also* ethics
costs, hidden, 183–187
creativity
Commanders and, 113, 121, 126, 130
Inspirers and, 14, 148–149, 157
criticism
Commanders and, 120, 121–122
Pleasers and, 35–36, 43–44, 47–48

decision making
Commanders and, 109–110
by Pleasers, 40
defensiveness, in Charmers, 97
denial, 34, 85
detail, attention to, 25, 158
diplomatic skills, of Pleasers, 29–31
discipline
of Charmers, 95–96
by Pleasers, 48–49, 53

Ebbers, Bernie, 34
Einstein, Albert, 190
emotion, 195–197
backlash, 174
blind spots in, 174–176
Charmer suppression of, 77, 78–81
Charmer views of, 49, 71–73, 97–98
Commanders and, 49, 104, 107–108
hidden costs of, 183–187

Pleasers and, 30–31, 40–41
Power Grid and, 7–11
empathy, 27
entrepreneurs, 103
envy
of Inspirers, 141, 152–154, 162–163
in Pleasers, 56–57
ethics
Charmers and, 68–69, 76–77
Commanders and, 113
Inspirers and, 149–150, 169–170
evaluations. *See* performance evaluations; self-evaluation
expectations
Charmers and, 94, 96–98
Commanders and, 121
Extraordinary Circumstances (Cooper), 27–28

family systems, 4–6. *See also* family systems theory
changing, 146–148
of Charmers, 73–75
of Commanders, 110–113, 130–131
ideal balance of power in, 36
of Inspirers, 137–138, 144–149
internalization of power behaviors in, 2
of Pleasers, 36–39
power gene coding in, 19–20
self-evaluation of, 16, 178–179
family systems theory, 4–6, 144–145
formal styles and, 10
professional styles and, 5–6
fear
Charmers and, 12, 73, 94, 97–98
Commanders and, 13
of failure to change, 17
on the Power Grid, 8–9
feedback
Charmers and, 71, 88
Commanders and, 119
for Inspirers, 143, 159

Index

Ford, Henry, 98
formal styles, 10–11, 13, 14. *See also*
    Commanders; Inspirers
freedom, 142–143, 146, 148
Freud, Sigmund, 4

Gardner, Gerald, 73–74
General Systems Theory, 4
Get Out of My Life, But First Could You
    Drive Me and Cheryl to the Mall?
    (Wolf), 146–148
group dynamics, 3, 10–11
    Charmers and, 86–89
    Commanders and, 102–103, 106–
        108
    definition of, 10
    Inspirers and, 140

hidden costs, 183–187
hierarchy
    Commanders and, 110–113
    Inspirers and, 140
    Pleasers and, 43–44
honesty, 193–195
hope, 139

image, Pleasers and, 49
impatience, 108–109
incentives
    Charmers and, 65–66, 96
    Commanders and, 121–122
    Inspirers and, 140, 149–150, 160
independence, 142–143, 157
influence
    of Charmers, 64–65
    of Inspirers, 136–137
informal styles, 9–10, 11–12. *See also*
    Charmers; Pleasers
innovation
    backlash against, 167–168
    Commanders and, 121
    Inspirers and, 138–139, 148–149,
        160, 167–168

Inspirers, 13–14, 135–171
    altruism in, 37–38
    big picture view of, 143–144
    blind spots of, 140–144, 175, 187
    as bosses, 158–162
    burnout in, 144
    case studies on, 151–154, 161–162,
        165–166, 169–170
    charisma of, 136–137
    Charmer bosses and, 86–89
    as entrepreneurs, 103
    family background of, 144–149
    leadership by, 137–138
    listening skills of, 28
    mission focus of, 27
    as peers, 162–166
    Pleaser envy of, 56–57
    politics and, 140–141
    practicality and, 158, 164–165
    prevalence of, 135
    reconditioning for, 178–181, 182–183,
        185–187
    red tape and, 142–143
    strengths of, 136–140
    as subordinates, 166–170
    in transitions, 41
    tunnel vision of, 141
    vision of, 138–139
instincts, 2
interaction styles
    of Charmers, 12, 78–80, 84, 85
    of Commanders, 13
    Commanders and, 106–107
    of Inspirers, 14, 139–140
    of Pleasers, 11–12, 27–28
    strategic pauses and, 181–183
intolerance, 107–108
intuition, in Pleasers, 27–28
iPhone, 143
It Doesn't Take a Hero (Schwarzkopf), 107

Jack: Straight from the Gut (Welch), 102
Jobs, Steve, 143

Index

Johnson, Bill, 69
Johnson, Roy, 108
Jolie, Angelina, 63
judgment, 10–11, 14, 197

Kennedy, John F., 98
Koepp, Stephen, 69

Laing, R. D., 144
likability, Pleasers and, 11–12
listening skills
    of Charmers, 84, 86–89, 96
    of Commanders, 116–117
    of Inspirers, 140
    of Pleasers, 28, 30–31
loyalty
    of Commanders, 107
    Commanders and, 131
    of Pleasers, 34–35

Machiavelli, Niccoló, 64
Madoff, Bernie, 5
Mead, Margaret, 4, 135
meaning making, 13–14
mentors, 140
Minuchin, Salvador, 5, 144
modeling, 137–138, 149–150, 169–170
morality, 15. See also ethics
Mother Teresa, 26
motivation. See incentives
Myers-Briggs Type Indicator, 14–15

organizational backlash, 167–168

Parental Alienation Syndrome (PAS),
    73–74
patience, 23, 108–109
Patton, George S., 119
peers
    Charmers as, 89–91
    Commanders as, 125–129
    Inspirers as, 162–166
    Pleasers as, 53–57

performance evaluations
    Commanders and, 120, 124–125
    Inspirers and, 160, 161–162
    by Pleasers, 48–49
    Pleasers and, 35–36, 43–44
perspective, 174–175, 184
Pleasers, 11–12, 25–61
    authority and, 67
    blind spots of, 31–36, 175, 186
    as bosses, 48–53
    boundary issues of, 53–54
    bullies and, 32–33
    career transitions and, 40–41
    case studies of, 18–19, 42–44, 51–53,
        56–57, 59–61
    Commander bosses and, 122–125
    diplomatic skills of, 29–31
    family background of, 36–39
    Inspirers and, 158, 165–166
    intuitive abilities of, 27–28
    listening skills of, 28
    loyalty of, 34–35
    as peers, 53–57
    performance evaluations and, 35–36
    political savvy of, 166
    prevalence of, 26
    process focus of, 68
    reconditioning for, 178–181, 182–183,
        185–187
    self-advocacy by, 31–32
    self-doubt in, 33–34
    strengths of, 26–31, 41
    as subordinates, 57–61
    work ethic of, 28–29
pleasure seeking, 175
political savvy, Inspirers and, 140–141,
    152–153, 159, 162–163, 166
power
    contagiousness of, 197–198
    definition of, 6
    establishing imbalances in, 9
    flow of in families, 4–6
    reflecting on, 198–199

power (*continued*)
  relationship with self and, 6–7
  turning points, 185, 186, 190–191,
    195–196
  wielding your, 193–199
power genes. *See also* reconditioning
  coding of, 19–20
  common concerns about, 16–17
  definition of, 7
  influence of, 4
  influence of on careers, 18–19
  snap judgments about, 10–11, 14,
    197
Power Grid, 4, 7–11
  acting on, 173–191
  blind spots and, 174–176
  Charmers on, 12
  getting started with, 22–23
  identifying hidden costs in, 183–187
  operating from multiple quadrants on,
    15–16
  Pleasers on, 11–12
  pros and cons of, 14–16
  reconditioning and, 173–191
  self-reflection on, 177–181
  time required for using, 16
  working with, 20–22
  x-axis, 9–11
  y-axis, 8–9
practicality, 158, 163–164
The Prince (Machiavelli), 64
problem solving, 66
process, Charmers and, 68–69

reconditioning, 21, 173–191
  case studies on, 178–181, 182–183,
    185–187, 188–189
  identifying hidden costs in, 183–187
  power quadrant identification in,
    177–181
  practicing new habits in, 187–189
  process for, 176–177
  strategic pauses in, 181–183

reflection
  Charmers and, 109
  Commanders and, 109–110
  identifying hidden costs through,
    183–187
  identifying power style with, 177–181
  identifying strengths with, 176
  self-, 5–6
regulatory roles, 25–26
resentment
  in Commanders, 126
  in Pleasers, 40–41
resilience, of Commanders, 104–105
resistance, 158, 164, 167–168
respect, 198
  Charmers and, 74–75
  Commanders and, 107
  Inspirers and, 145
  Pleasers and, 54
responsibility, Pleasers and, 29
risk taking
  by Charmers, 70–71, 85
  Commanders and, 126
  by Inspirers, 138–139
Rogers, Carl, 4
Rowley, Coleen, 28

Satir, Virginia, 4, 144
scarcity, sense of in Pleasers, 12, 26, 29,
    33–34, 36–39
Schwarzkopf, Norman, 101, 107
Scott, George C., 119
Scudder, Stevens & Clark, 3
secrecy, 9
self-advocacy, by Pleasers, 31–32, 39,
    47–48
self-confidence
  of Charmers, 71, 90, 95
  of Commanders, 105–106, 125
  of Inspirers, 135, 137
self-evaluation, 16
  discomfort in, 17
  time for, 16

Index

self-sabotage, 197–198

Sinatra, Frank, 63, 67–68

Spitzer, Eliot, 5, 190

spontaneity, 14

status, Commander desire for, 102, 103, 107, 122–125

strategic pauses, 181–183

Strawberry, Darryl, 12, 63, 65–66, 70–71, 74–75

Straw: Finding My Way (Strawberry), 65–66

strengths, identifying, 176, 189

subordinates
 Charmers as, 94–98
 Charmers as bosses of, 84
 Commanders as, 129–131
 Inspirers as, 166–170
 Pleasers as, 57–59

success, definitions of, 3, 109–110

succession planning, 160

systems theory. *See* family systems

team building, 143–144

Thatcher, Margaret, 101

Thich Nhat Hanh, 26

transitions
 Charmers in, 75–77
 Commanders in, 112, 113–114
 Inspirers in, 149–150, 168–169
 Pleasers and, 40–41

transparency, 30

trust
 Charmers and, 69, 72, 74–75, 77, 91
 Inspirers and, 13
 Pleasers and, 11
 seeking, 8, 9
 self-, 198

turning points, 185, 186, 190–191, 195–196

Ungeheur, Frederick, 69

urgency, fostering, 9

The Virtues of Aging (Carter), 138

vision
 of Commanders, 109–110, 115–116
 of Inspirers, 138–139

Washington, George, 101

Watkins, Sherron, 28

Welch, Jack, 13, 101, 102, 105, 108, 111, 112

Wiener, Jon, 67–68

Wiesel, Elie, 26

Wolf, Anthony, 146–148

Woodman, Marion, 39

working styles
 of Charmers, 69–71, 80, 94
 of Inspirers, 144
 of Pleasers, 28–29, 185–186

WorldCom, 11, 25–26, 27–28, 34

ACKNOWLEDGMENTS

This book was born from the dedicated work of numerous clients around the world whose courageous search for the roots of their power styles revealed the foundational structure of this methodology. I cannot possibly list all the talented people who, through sharing their stories with me, have faced the ways that the power patterns they learned in their family systems have influenced their professional behavior. Let me simply say that you have all been my teachers, and my hope is that this book inspires others the way that you have inspired me.

I'd like to thank Linda Lowenthal, my wonderful agent at David Black, who has helped me bring my second book into the publishing world. Since the success of my first book, *The Authentic Career,* Linda has encouraged my evolving voice as an executive coach. Her professional support and positive energy have played a large part in my growth as an author. Thanks as well to Linda's colleague, Antonella Iannarino, who has helped us harness the power of technology to bring this methodology to a wider global audience.

I'd also like to thank my fabulous editor at Harvard Business Review Press, Ania Wieckowski, who has made refining this manuscript and publishing this book a delightful experience. Special thanks as well to Jacque Murphy, whose expertise in the final laps of the editing process helped me both refine and more clearly express my message. I'm also grateful for the insights from the members of the peer review committee at the Press, who lent their expertise and insight to this project as it evolved.

Acknowledgments

Some very special friends and colleagues are responsible for bringing this work from the corporate-coaching world into the publishing arena. To that end, I must begin by thanking Bronwyn Fryer, whose initial enthusiasm for this methodology led to the article in *Harvard Business Review* that sparked the expansion of this concept. I'd also like to thank Kirsten Sandberg, whose early editorial support helped me convey these concepts more effectively.

Special thanks to my friend and colleague Maria Nordone, who has supported me both personally and professionally as I have put these principles into practice in my life as well as my work. I'd also like to thank my brilliant colleague Judy Tschirgi, who gave me frank feedback based on her experience as both a senior executive and a caring mentor during this process. Thanks as well to Linda Munn for her formidable insights during the genesis of this project.

I'd also like to thank the rest of the team from Workplace Relationships who have helped me put these concepts into practice, including Tom Troy, Bob Schulman, Kimberley Euston, Nicole Woodard, and, of course, my wonderful assistant Mirella Cicio.

My heartfelt thanks go out to the late, great Adrienne Hall and the wonderful members of Women's Leadership Board at the Kennedy School at Harvard. These talented people lent their enthusiasm and support to this work in its early stages. Thanks as well to Amanda Pullinger, Anne Popkin, and the fabulous women from 100 Women in Hedge Funds for their ongoing support of my work.

There are some very special friends I'd like to mention because their ongoing presence in my life has been critical to the creation of this work: Nan and Lee Corbin, Brian Hull, Loreen Arbus, Bruce Larson, Lara Warner, Roelfein Kuijpers, Mindy Schwartz, Tracey Miele, Susan Dunn, Betsy Boruchoff, Steve Yatko, Keith Green, Becky and Sohail Sayeg, Mark Krug, P.J. and Ron Greiner, Rob Craddock, Sharon and Dave Clarton, Steve and the late Karen Brown, and Vickie Parker.

Finally, I'd like to acknowledge the members of my immediate family who have shaped me and loved me: my mother and father, Nancy and Perry Craddock, who have waited patiently between visits while I finished this project. My deepest debt of gratitude goes to my wonderful fiancé, Charles Schneider, for sharing my hopes, listening to my dreams, and loving me through it all.

ABOUT THE AUTHOR

Maggie Craddock is an executive coach who has worked with clients across the professional spectrum, from executives climbing the corporate ladder to *Fortune 500* CEOs. She has been featured on CNBC and National Public Radio and quoted in national publications including *Newsweek,* the *Wall Street Journal,* and the *Los Angeles Times.* Maggie is the author of *The Authentic Career,* which has been featured at conferences around the world. She has also written nationally syndicated articles on behavioral dynamics in the workplace, and her work has been discussed in *O: The Oprah Magazine.*

Maggie speaks around the world on workplace issues, with audiences ranging from leadership conferences for her corporate clients, graduates from business schools including Harvard and Columbia, and professional organizations including 100 Women in Hedge Funds and The Women's Leadership Board for Harvard's Kennedy School of Government.

Before building her executive coaching practice, Maggie worked for over a decade in the financial services industry. As a buy side portfolio manager at Scudder, Stevens & Clark, she received two Lipper Awards for top fund performance. On the sell side, Maggie served as a National Director of Consultant Relations at Sanford C. Bernstein, representing the firm across all asset classes, including emerging markets, domestic and international fixed income, and domestic and international equity to major consultant and pension fund clients across the United States.

Maggie got her BA in economics from Smith College and received an MSc in Economics from the London School of Economics, specializing in capital markets. After leaving Wall Street, Maggie pursued formal counseling training to augment her business experience and develop her own approach to executive coaching. She received an MSW from New York University and went on to become an Ackerman certified family therapist. Maggie is also a graduate of Wharton's Advanced Management Program.

In her spare time, Maggie pursues her passionate interest in visiting the great trees of the world. She has traveled around the globe to learn about, photograph, and sketch trees in national forests, botanical gardens, and along nature trails. Maggie lives in Exton, Pennsylvania, with her fiancé, Charles Schneider.

For additional information or to contact Maggie, please visit www.workplacerelationships.com.